BRIAN SIEMENS

Money: What I Wish I Knew When I Was Younger

A Cautionary Tale & Lessons Learned For Teens & Young Adults

Copyright © 2020 by Brian Siemens

All rights reserved. No part of this publication may be reproduced, stored or transmitted in any form or by any means, electronic, mechanical, photocopying, recording, scanning, or otherwise without written permission from the publisher. It is illegal to copy this book, post it to a website, or distribute it by any other means without permission.

Brian Siemens has no responsibility for the persistence or accuracy of URLs for external or third-party Internet Websites referred to in this publication and does not guarantee that any content on such Websites is, or will remain, accurate or appropriate.

First edition

*This book was professionally typeset on Reedsy.
Find out more at reedsy.com*

Contents

Preface	iv
Author's Note	vii
1 Feeding the Monster	1
2 Lifestyle vs. Quality of Life	6
3 Growing Up	10
4 The Beginning of Bad Habits	14
5 Dream Big, Execute Small	19
6 Impulse Buying	27
7 Beware of Credit Cards	41
8 Be Careful with Student Loans	55
9 An Introduction to Your New Best Friend: Money Management...	62
10 Final Tips	75
11 The End Game: Where It All Leads	96
Acknowledgements	101
About the Author	103

Preface

"It's what you learn after you know it all that counts."
— **John Wooden,** Legendary UCLA men's basketball coach

"Hi! My name is Brian and I'm a financial idiot." If I were attending a meeting or class for those dysfunctional with money or with a money management disorder, that is how I would introduce myself. I would continue, "I have spent the majority of the past twenty years—my entire earning life—making bad decision after bad decision with respect to money. I have caved to every whim or impulse to spend with absolutely no thought about or regard to the impact on my current situation or the future. I am here because the struggle is real and exhausting and I can't take it anymore. I must change my ways with money! My happiness depends on it."

You may think that I'm exaggerating or being a bit dramatic, but as you'll soon read, I'm not. My situation really was that bad, only at the time I didn't completely know it or understand it. I just knew I was running in circles, going nowhere, and had realized that some things needed to change. But I really didn't comprehend the gravity of the situation. That's pretty common for most of us—true understanding usually comes with hindsight and reflection once we've recognized or admitted there's a problem and we are driven to seeking a solution to whatever is causing us pain.

That understanding is what you'll get here. I have spent countless hours reviewing and reliving the mistakes of the past and what I could have and should have done differently. I wonder how things might be different today if I had? Not that I would necessarily change any of it. I believe there is a reason and purpose for everything, and sharing my situation with you is that purpose.

My one goal is to help you avoid the mistakes, stresses, and setbacks I have endured by sharing my struggles and how I overcame them. Many if not most of the stories I'm going to share are somewhat embarrassing to my adult self. But that's okay—I can take it. It's worth being embarrassed if my story helps you.

I am not a licensed professional when it comes to personal finance. I don't have any fancy designations or certifications behind my name. I only have a title that I've given to myself: I've recently been calling myself a financial coach, although I think a financial *educator* is more accurate.

I can't legally tell you what financial products to invest your money in or advise you on what strategy is best for your situation. That kind of advice has to be left to a licensed financial advisor.

What I *can* do is provide guidance and advice on what financial *behaviors* will and will not lead to success based on my nearly thirty years of experience. I can help you with your everyday decision-making when it comes to your money, help you focus on the big picture of achieving your goals, and help you understand why sound personal finance is so important to your long-term happiness and success.

But here's the catch: I can't put anything into action for you. I can provide all the hard-knocks stories, all the lessons learned, the what to do and the what not to do, but the only person who can actually put this advice into action and make the right choices is *you*. The only way for you to know if the tips and guidance I provide actually work is for you to implement them.

There's something here for everybody. If you're just starting off or already in a good place, then there is plenty here to inspire you to keep at it. If you're already on shaky ground and need to get on track, then there is plenty of information for your situation as well.

Who am I to give anyone money management advice considering my track record? Well, just as much—if not more—valuable information comes from someone's failures and setbacks as from their successes and achievements. And yes, there is an element of success to my story, too.

All I'm asking is for you not to be too quick to discount anything I'm telling you and to try the things I'm suggesting. Stick with me. I promise there's a payoff for you! I've written this book in an effort to provide valuable information that will yield immediate results. Small, subtle changes can create big results, and quickly. If my advice works, pass it on; if it doesn't, let me know why.

Author's Note

When I set out to write this book, my idea was to put on paper my struggles with money, the mistakes I made, my lack of preparedness for future emergencies, the self-inflicted stress, the missed opportunities, and my diminished quality of life. The only goal was to help someone, anyone, avoid my mistakes so they could realize a better quality of life that is available to them right now. That was and still is my singular goal for you.

I knew it would be a difficult proposition to convince you to prepare for the worst, save money for a rainy day, and imagine what bad times would look like if you hadn't experienced any of that already. After all, we were in the middle of a booming economy with a record-high stock market and record-low unemployment. Times were good; for many, times were great. Add on to that the fact that many of us, no matter our age, really don't consider the worst possible scenario until we get punched in the face with it.

And that's exactly what happened. Things turned bad in a hurry. We were blindsided by something called COVID-19. Never in my wildest dreams would I have imagined that toward the end of the writing of this book, we'd experience a pandemic that would possibly transform our lives for the foreseeable future and would provide a real-life experience for *everyone* that would reinforce the message I was sharing.

In a matter of months, we went from a booming economy to

a nationwide shutdown and a potential depression. From the best unemployment numbers in history to the worst. Record claims for unemployment assistance and a tanking stock market. Things became so dire that the government passed a $2 trillion stimulus package to help people pay rent, buy groceries, and pay their bills. As of the writing of this, Congress is discussing the possibility of more stimulus programs.

Many of the lost jobs may never come back, and if they do, I imagine that the job market will be more competitive than ever with those who lost their jobs seeking new ones alongside the thousands of new college and high school graduates who are now sitting on the sidelines, waiting and hoping for their opportunity.

If you were one of the fortunate ones who did not lose your job but you are also not prepared for life without a steady income for some time, you must now make difficult decisions between your financial responsibilities and your health and well-being, between being able to continue to pay for housing, transportation, groceries, etc. versus being able to stay healthy and avoid the potential consequences of venturing out daily.

For those of you who were prepared to absorb the financial implications of something so unexpected and devastating (and I assume that number is low), that's fantastic! You're much further ahead than most people. Use this book to smooth out any rough edges you may have in your money management techniques and keep up the good work.

For those of you who are on the other side of experiencing the stress and financial hardship of a pandemic, use that experience and this book as a building block of preparedness, emergency planning, and responsible money management that will serve you in the future. You know—more so than ever before—that it's impossible to know what the future holds.

1

Feeding the Monster

"If you live for having it all, what you have is never enough."
— **Vicki Robin,** Co-author of *Your Money or Your Life: 9 Steps to Transforming Your Relationship with Money and Achieving Financial Independence*

For as long as I can remember, my goal in life was to acquire as many possessions as I could. I thought the more I had, the happier I would be and the more successful I would feel. All through my twenties and early thirties, no matter what town I lived in, I would drive through the nicest neighborhoods looking at the houses and the cars in the driveways, wondering how people got there and imagining how happy they must be. Would I ever be able to have that?

I used to think things like, *Once I have this, I'll start saving money; once I get in that position, I'll start giving. Because then I'll have everything I want for myself, and I'll no longer have a reason not to save or give. I'll have the newly constructed house with more bedrooms than we need, because it is critical to have one or two unused bedrooms so that guests can come to stay a couple times a year or even less often. No sleeping on the couch or a blow-up mattress at my house! And what about the dedicated office with the nice desk so I can go in there and sit a couple hours a month to open mail and pay the bills? And then there are the cars. Cars have to fit the house and the neighborhood.* My thoughts kept going, but you get the idea. All of this was going to make me happy…or so I thought.

There was only one way to fuel my desire for more possessions and to upgrade the possessions I already had: make more money. So every three or four years, I would begin looking for a new job basically doing the same thing I was already doing. I would cash in on the experience gained from my current job by finding the same job or a similar job with slightly more responsibility that paid five or ten thousand dollars more per year. That would satisfy my desire to up my lifestyle by acquiring new and better possessions, at least for the time being. Then a few years later, I would do it again.

I wouldn't even consider a job or send a résumé unless it paid more than my current job. That was the only requirement. Career path or opportunity for promotion didn't matter, because I wasn't going to be there long enough. Whether or not I liked the job or the work didn't matter, because I could do anything for a couple of years if it meant more money. Besides, work wasn't something that dictated happiness, or so I thought. It was just the money. A good culture at the office? Nope. Compatibility with management? Nope. Money? YES, YES, YES!

I also never took into account if the potential bump in salary was actually enough of an increase in my take-home pay to justify the effort of transitioning to a new job. What if the small raise bumped me to a new tax bracket, thus eating up the gain in my salary? For example, a single person making $9,876 to $40,125 in 2020 pays a 12% federal tax, while a single person making $40,126 to $85,525 has their federal taxes jump to 22%.

Say someone is making $40,000. A simple calculation of $40,000 multiplied by a tax rate of .12 leaves $35,200. At first glance, a job offer of $46,000 looks pretty appealing. But another quick calculation of the new salary multiplied by the new tax rate of .22 (since the salary is now above the $40,125 max income of the 12% tax bracket) reveals a federal income tax of $10,120, leaving only $35,880.

What originally looks good on the surface—a 15% increase in annual income—is really only an increase of $680 for the entire year. If that person is paid biweekly (26 paychecks per year), we're talking about only $26.15 more per pay period. And we haven't even considered deductions like social security, Medicare, and FICA tax. Increases to those could actually result in a biweekly take-home pay of less money than before.

If you enter the job market in high school or shortly after, when you are likely making less money than the example above, the same can still hold true. Maybe you got a part-time job at a local coffee shop with a great family atmosphere working 20 hours a week at $9.15 an hour. That equates to roughly $9,516 annually. Multiplying that amount by the 10% (minimum) tax rate leaves around $8,865.

You later hear that Starbucks is hiring part-time help starting at $10 an hour, so you apply and get the job. Your annual income increases to $10,400, but also bumps you to the 12% tax bracket. Now your annual federal taxes are $1,248, leaving you $9,152 for a net gain of $287 over your old job.

After a couple of weeks at Starbucks, you begin to question your decision. The customer traffic is five times what it was at the mom-and-pop shop. You and your coworkers are more stressed due to the fast-paced pressure and as a result aren't all that friendly to each other. In fairness to Starbucks, I'm not a coffee drinker, don't frequent Starbucks, and have never worked there. But you get the point. Is the meager bump in money worth it and should it have been the only factor you considered?

After years of job-hopping for no other reason than to make more money, I achieved the lifestyle I had been seeking. I was in my early forties, and I had made it and I was finally going to be happy. But what I had failed to realize was that a certain lifestyle (which was all I had been chasing) was just a small piece of the big equation of happiness. I had been lured into thinking small and not seeing the big picture of life.

What I realized was that even though I had achieved what seemed like a much greater lifestyle, I still was not completely happy. And unfortunately, I was still unable to figure out what would lead to the happiness I was seeking. It's an empty feeling. You've worked hard to get the things that you believe will make you happy, and in the end, it doesn't work the way you thought. What was it all for? I'm sure I had been told many times that money was not everything and would not necessarily lead to happiness, but I'm also sure I didn't always listen to that or even believe it.

So again, I quit my job. This time, I did it before having something that paid more lined up. I just quit. As I began looking for my next job, for the first time I had a second criterion in addition to making more money: I was going to give working from home a try. This was the first time that compensation alone wasn't going to cut it. I had hit my breaking point. Going to work at a job I didn't like had become unbearable no matter how much money I was making. However, I thought if I did the same job—in the comfortable surroundings of my home office—I might be happy.

But as I read the job descriptions of the jobs I was applying for, I soon realized that it was more than the office environment that I needed to escape. It was the work itself. Whether I was working in an office or doing the same job at home, I wasn't going to be satisfied or happy.

In that moment I was coming to realize two things: first, no matter the money and the amount of possessions, my level of happiness was not going to increase; second, I was never going to be happy as long as I continued to do the same work I had always done.

2

Lifestyle vs. Quality of Life

"Fact: If standard of living is your number-one objective, quality of life almost never improves. But if quality of life is your number-one objective, standard of living invariably improves."
 — **Zig Ziglar,** Author and motivational speaker

After so many years, my narrow thinking was starting to expand, but I still couldn't put my finger on what I was looking for. I started to research happiness and life. What were the true secrets to happiness? Eventually I came across the phrase "quality of life." I had heard the phrase many times before, but here I was at 41 never having fully understood what it meant or even having given it much thought.

If you had asked me if I had a good quality of life, I would have said, "Sure. I have a nice home, nice cars, nice clothes, get to travel a couple times a year, eat out when I want, go out with friends, and so on." I would have listed all the things that I had eventually learned made up a good lifestyle. But what I had also learned was that a nice lifestyle is only a single piece of what makes up a good quality of life.

You see, your lifestyle is more about how you feel about your day-to-day life: how nice the house or apartment you live in is, how nice the car you drive is, how nice the clothes you wear are, how nice the places you eat are, how nice the furnishings in your house are, and on and on.

When we make lifestyle our sole focus or the majority of our focus, we neglect nearly every other aspect of our quality of life. That's what I did! Collectively, we end up living beyond our means. We buy more house than we can afford and more car than we can afford, we wear clothes we really cannot afford, we frequent dining establishments we cannot afford, and we socialize in places we cannot afford. And in doing so, we commit ourselves to a great lifestyle, but an overall lower quality of life.

Our quality of life is an overall feeling that takes into account many other factors than just our day-to-day lifestyle. It consists of financial security, job satisfaction, family life, health, safety, and stress level.

Are you secure in a financial sense? Do you have enough income or savings to cover all of your expenses, any emergencies, and some goals you may have? Are you content with your job? Are you healthy? Do you feel safe inside your home and its surroundings? What is your level of stress on a scale of one to ten?

What happens is that so many of us get caught up in our lifestyle—on *possessions*—that we neglect all of the other areas that are critical to having a good or even great quality of life.

We find ourselves miserable at work. Like many, I used to

live for 5:00 pm on Friday afternoons when I could take off for the weekend. I hated being at my job no matter how much money I made. Then by the time 4:00 pm on Sundays rolled around, I was already beginning to dread going back to work on Monday morning. Many times, I had a difficult time even enjoying my free time away from work because all I could think about was going back. I would count down my vacation days. As soon as I was three to four days into a week off from work, I would begin thinking about how my time was almost over even though I had another three or four days remaining.

All of us do things to jeopardize our health and safety. We cut corners on what we eat because less-healthy foods are less expensive than more-nutritious, higher-quality foods. Some of us drive on tires that are worn out and way overdue for replacement. When there's a financial emergency, our stress level goes through the roof as we go further into credit card debt or search for a friend or relative from whom to borrow money. In my case, I had massive stress due to my work.

I was fortunate that I was able to keep the demands of my desired lifestyle and my unhappiness and stress from work from impacting my home life and my relationships with my wife and children. But I *was* letting my desired lifestyle be the overriding factor of my happiness. Looking back, it was never going to work.

Whether we are consciously choosing lifestyle instead of a better overall quality of life or just confused about the difference between the two, the statistics show us the consequences:

· 37.8 million households are paying more for housing than they can afford (i.e., spending more than 30% of their income for housing) according to the 2019 "State of the Nation's Housing" report published by the Joint Center for Housing Studies of Harvard University.

· Nearly 30% of Americans say they have nothing saved in an emergency fund according to a Bankrate Financial Security Index published in 2019.

· 28% of Americans would find it difficult to cover an unexpected expense of $400 according to the Federal Reserve's 2019 "Report on the Economic Well-Being of U.S. Households."

· According to the same Federal Reserve report released in 2019, 25% of Americans skipped necessary medical care like going to the doctor or a dentist because they couldn't afford the cost.

· A record 7 million Americans are 3 months behind on their car payments according to a 2019 report from the Federal Reserve Bank of New York's Center for Microeconomic Data.

New statistics like these pop up constantly. In fact, as I write this, another one was just announced:

· 64% of Americans have less than $10,000 saved for retirement and will likely retire broke according to a 2019 survey from GOBankingRates.com.

Is there any doubt at all that we as a society are putting lifestyle first and neglecting our overall quality of life? But how do you keep yourself from falling into this horrible trap?

3

Growing Up

"Experience is a master teacher, even when it's not our own."
— **Gina Greenlee**, Best-selling author, speaker, teacher, and coach

This is a story of the hard way. Not hard luck, but the hard way. Be sure not to confuse the two. Hard *luck* is when something bad happens through no fault of your own. Like most of us, I experienced what could be described as some hard luck. I had some unfortunate incidents to overcome, but few of us get through childhood without some hard luck. We can let it defeat us, or we can take away the good parts and come out better for it.

On the other hand, the hard *way* is self-inflicted. It involves lessons learned from difficult or painful experiences that we brought on ourselves by our own choices. Many times, we choose to put ourselves on a collision course with the hard way after ignoring warnings from others who have experienced their own hard way. Experiences or encounters may shape our outlook or desires, but ultimately our own choices are what carve our path and lead us down this hard way.

The sooner we choose to learn from the experience of those who have gone before us, the better off we will be. But the sad truth is that most of us are too stubborn to take this to heart. This is my story of the hard way, a story I hope you will learn from and use as a guide for making better choices.

I was born in Kansas, but my family relocated to the town of Bartlesville, Oklahoma when I was three years old. Bartlesville is a town approximately 40 minutes north of Tulsa with about 35,000 people. It never shrinks, never grows. It's odd that way. It was and always has been known for one thing: Phillips Petroleum, or Phillips 66. It was a huge company for such a small town. And if you lived in Bartlesville and didn't work there, I have no idea why you were there or what you did.

By the time I was six years old, we were a family of six living in a three-bedroom, one bathroom, 1,100-square-foot house. Being a small town with a large petroleum and oil company, there was a lot of money in Bartlesville. Some families had a lot of it; others not so much. It was not difficult to see what my friends and classmates had and compare it to what I had. Don't get me wrong—we were not poor. We were middle-class, but middle-class was not the same in Bartlesville as in most other places of similar size.

Both my mom and dad were college graduates. My mom was a registered nurse. My dad... Well, I'm not quite sure what he did. I know he worked in insurance and a few other things before settling in at Phillips. Other than going to school, I was involved in sports: I played soccer, baseball, and basketball with my dad coaching all of them. I was not very talented athletically, but I tried hard. I was always very competitive—growing up with a brother eleven-and-a-half months younger than I was fueled that competitive nature.

I attended St. John's Catholic School, a private school, from kindergarten to the sixth grade. Yes, a middle-class kid educated at a private school. What's to complain about, right? *It must have been so rough.* I get it, but I didn't even know it was a private school or what a private school was. All I could see was that my friends were wearing Nikes and Levi's with their uniform shirts and I was wearing Fast Bak tennis shoes and Toughskins jeans. You've probably never heard of either one. Google it!

Today, I get it. As a father of three children and two stepchildren, it makes sense to provide them with what they need in the most cost-efficient way. But back then, I was always asking myself why I couldn't have what the other kids had.

My parents upgraded to a new, larger home with a larger mortgage. Immediately after getting settled in, we left on a road trip, our annual summer vacation. Upon our return, my parents separated; they eventually divorced when I was in the sixth grade. My dad moved out of the house when they separated and gave up any claim to the house during the divorce, leaving the new mortgage to my mom. As part of the arrangement, my dad paid child support and provided medical insurance for us kids through his employer.

Instead of a dual-income home with one house, one set of utilities, and one set of goals, everything was now divided. It was now two parents paying for two separate residences. With that came more money spent on rent or mortgage, utilities, insurance, taxes, and such.

My middle-school years were spent living with my dad and my younger brother. My other younger brother and sister lived with our mom. By this time, we had graduated to Knights of the Round Table polo shirts and Wrangler jeans. A far cry from the Polo brand shirts and Guess jeans our friends were wearing… I was still comparing myself to others and focusing on what I did not have.

After a year and a half of living with my father and alternating weekends between my younger siblings coming to stay with us and my brother and I going to stay at my mom's, my three siblings and I were reunited with my mother toward the end of my eighth-grade year. While I may not have realized it at the time or fully understood why, looking back, it's obvious why money was tight, especially for my mother. There were a few dollars to spend here and there to go to a movie on a Friday night or go to the mall with friends on a Saturday afternoon, but nothing consistent. There was no weekly allowance for doing chores.

I learned early on that I was going to have to work if I wanted more.

4

The Beginning of Bad Habits

"The best cure for one's bad tendencies is to see them in action in another person."
— **Alain de Botton**, Philosopher and author

I understood that I needed to make money in order to buy the things I wanted. My first job came from Mr. Cole, my seventh-grade science teacher, when I was fourteen years old. I would play ball in the neighborhood, usually across the street from Mr. Cole's house with the other neighborhood kids, including Mr. Cole's two sons.

One evening, Mr. Cole asked if I would be interested in mowing his yard if he paid me since he didn't have a mower of his own at the time. This was my first chance to make some money, so I jumped all over it. Of course I told him I would do it! He offered me $10 for the whole yard, but I'd have to use my own mower.

As often as he would let me, I would push my mom's mower and carry the gas can two blocks to Mr. Cole's house. His backyard was a pretty good size, so it took a little more gas than the mower's tank would hold, and without the gas can, I would come up short. I'd mow his yard and return to my mom's with the mower, gas can, and $10 I had earned. For a kid who didn't have much, it seemed like a pretty sweet deal. Ironically, a few years later, Mr. Cole started a successful landscaping and lawn service that is still in business today.

That $10 was cool for a while, but it didn't keep me satisfied for long. It only went so far in paying for junk food and supporting my new hobby, which was collecting baseball cards. It was 1989, and the baseball card boom was just beginning, with everyone chasing the hottest thing: the Ken Griffey Jr. rookie card. There were new card companies popping up everywhere, producing multiple brands of cards in mass quantities. There were three card shops in my town, and it seemed like there was one in every other nearby town, too. Today, there might not be three shops in the entire state.

When I turned fifteen, there weren't many places to find a decent-paying job. (You generally had to be sixteen to apply.) But one place that was hiring was the local newspaper. I inquired about a paper route and found out that there would be one in my neighborhood a few blocks from my house that would soon be available. I spent a few days training with the current carrier, and then the route was mine.

Every day, I delivered fifty papers to houses on two streets that were four blocks away from my house. I was responsible for having the papers on the porches of my customers by 5:00 pm on weekdays and by 7:00 am on weekends. I earned $100 per month from the newspaper company along with the occasional tip.

I say "the porches" because that's what my predecessor did—since he lived on one of the two streets on the route, he walked the route and dropped each paper on each customer's front porch. Because that's what he did and what the customers were used to, that's what I did, for a while at least.

Because I lived four blocks away from my route, most of the time I rode a bike to deliver the papers. Since I could not accurately reach the front porch of the houses from the street, I would ride in and out of each driveway to hit the porch. You can imagine the time and difficulty involved in doing this on a ten-speed bicycle. Many times, it was a tight fit to get close enough to the porch *and* at the same time make a successful turnaround to get out of the driveway and back to the street.

As soon as I realized that there was no immediate financial benefit to making this effort, I stopped delivering to the front door. I was not earning any tips or extra compensation from doing that during the first few months, so I simply began throwing the papers to the driveway of each house as I cruised down the middle of the street. Had I continued providing better service up to and through the holidays that first year, who knows? Maybe it would have paid dividends with some nice tips.

This is the point where things began to go sideways for me when it came to managing money. Again, I was only fifteen and didn't really know any better, but it just goes to show that if we get started on the wrong foot, we can easily develop habits that can take years or a lifetime to overcome, if we ever overcome them at all.

Each month, I had the responsibility of collecting monthly payments from the customers. Looking back, it was questionable in and of itself why the newspaper company would make that the responsibility of a kid, but that's what it was. I got to keep one-third of the payment, which in my case was $2 from each customer.

So sometime during the month, I would go door-to-door asking for $6 from each customer. You can imagine the time this took! Sometimes they were home; sometimes they weren't. Sometimes they had the cash; sometimes they didn't. But one way or another, at the end of every month, it was my responsibility to turn in $200 to the newspaper company.

You can probably see where this is going. Obviously, it would have made the most sense to secure the first $200 and make the payment to the newspaper company and then collect the remaining money owed from the customers to pay myself. Of course, this was the exact opposite of what I did.

My fifteen-year old brain never thought that far ahead. I never thought, *What will I do at the end of the month if I don't have the money to pay the newspaper company? Where will I get that money?* I just knew that I had money. I had cash in hand that could be spent *right then*.

So naturally, the first $100 I collected, I spent on myself. Immediately. And I did this over and over again, every month. I'd go to my favorite baseball card shop and buy a couple of boxes of card packs to open and spend the rest on junk food at convenience stores. Then toward the end of the month when I was supposed to pay the newspaper company, I'd scramble to come up with the money—I'd make one last round to the doors of my customers and then look to borrow the rest, promising to pay it back once I had collected it.

So there I was at age fifteen, seeking immediate gratification by paying myself first, impulsively buying anything and everything I had the money to get my hands on, and already learning to spend money that wasn't really mine, thus creating debt for myself.

While there were a lot worse things I could have been spending my money on at the time, the real problem was the bad habits I was developing. Impulse buying, not saving anything, not focusing on my short- or long-term goals. Bad habits that caused setback after setback and took me nearly twenty years to break.

5

Dream Big, Execute Small

"It must be borne in mind that the tragedy of life doesn't lie in not reaching your goal. The tragedy lies in having no goals to reach."
— **Benjamin E. Mays**, Minister and civil rights leader

I finally turned sixteen, the age required to get a real job, and a hundred bucks a month wasn't cutting it anymore. By this time, I had already determined that after high school I would be going to college. It was a big, long-term goal.

Both of my parents had gone to college, but it was never stressed in my home as something you had to do—it was just ingrained in me that I was going to college. I thought there was no other way I'd be able to earn the kind of income that was necessary for the lifestyle I hoped to one day have. I also knew I didn't want to live in my hometown for the rest of my life, a small town where so many relied on what I considered to be only one good employment option. While a few of my grade school and high school friends planned on remaining there (and still do), most wanted to move on after high school, myself included. We wanted to look for more choices and opportunities, which college would provide.

But while college was a long-term goal, that's all it was to me. It was down the road and certainly not a priority. I guess I thought it was just going to magically happen on its own. My only thinking was that if I could get a second job, I could buy more baseball cards, junk food, and other things I later came to realize I didn't need. It turns out that the things I thought I needed weren't really needs at all. It wasn't until I learned the difference between "wants" and "needs" that I recognized that my needs were already being met by my mother and that all of the things I was blowing my money on were just wants. (We'll take a deeper dive into the concept of "wants" and "needs" in the next chapter.)

I knew my mother wasn't going to be able to help me pay for college. For very complicated reasons, my dad was no longer in the picture, so my mom had become a single mother of four. And as a single mother of four, it was difficult enough to take care of the things we needed. Paying for college for one child—let alone four—wasn't going to happen. My siblings and I all knew that. Unfortunately, knowing that fact was not enough for me to change my habits in order to actually get myself to college by focusing on saving money.

Still focused on short-term gratification, I set out to find a job as close to my house as possible. I would need to ride my bike or walk everywhere because saving money for a car had not been a priority. I applied to a Pizza Hut a mile from my house and got a job starting out as a dishwasher. Minimum wage back then was $5.25 an hour. As a bonus, they offered me a personal pan pizza every night I worked for only 50 cents. Great deal!

So I was coming home from school every afternoon, rolling my papers, wrapping them in rubber bands, delivering them to my customer's driveways, going home and washing the black ink off my hands, and then walking, riding a bike, or bumming a ride to Pizza Hut to wash dishes.

The chemicals that were required in the rinse water for the dishes would dry out my hands so badly that they would crack, bleed, and scab over at times. I finally learned to wear gloves, as I had originally been instructed to do. But the misery of the job was quickly forgotten when payday came. I would immediately cash my check and—you guessed it!—head to the baseball card shop or the convenience store or some fast-food restaurant.

As for my goal of going to college when I graduated, I clearly was not making the proper decisions that would lead to actually making that happen. What I've since learned is that I had a big goal, but no direction to accomplish it. I had never considered the process involved. I had never set any short-term goals to support and back up my long-term goals.

When we set long-term, big-picture goals, they require incremental or baby steps in order to achieve them. You have to think big, but then you have to think small. In my case, college was big. *Huge,* really, since I was going to have to pay for it myself. Going small to support my big goal would have meant making biweekly deposits that coincided with each payday into a savings account earmarked for college only.

I should have had a monthly budget that would have shown me how much money I was expecting to make and then earmarked certain amounts for everything I wanted at the time.

That would have allowed me to limit what I was spending in order to ensure that I was meeting my savings goal. A budget for eating out, a budget for entertainment (which would have included collecting), and a budget for anything else I was spending money on.

But I never opened a checking or savings account during my high school years. I took my paychecks and cashed them and then blew the cash. With each job and more money came the urge to buy more. The idea of saving never crossed my mind. And if you had asked me if I had a budget or what one was, I would have looked at you as if you were speaking a foreign language.

Eventually, I looked for a new job that would pay a higher hourly wage and give me more hours. I gave little if any thought to the quality of the job or the work I would be doing. My only concern was whether or not it would sustain my growing desire to spend more money on things I didn't need.

As I continued to develop destructive habits regarding money and spending and as I closed in on my high school graduation, I finally began to focus on my goal of going to college. I was still not budgeting or saving, but I began applying to colleges and trying to navigate the road of securing funding to pay for college. I had learned about financial aid and loans for college, and *that* was going to be my way out.

I took the ACT twice. The first time, I scored the bare minimum that was required to be accepted into a state school. The second time, I did worse. I really shouldn't have bothered the second time—I knew I was in with my first score and had made absolutely no effort to improve upon it. I was up way too late the night before and got only four hours of sleep. I didn't even want to go take it again.

I was accepted to my dream school, the University of Oklahoma (OU). I applied for no other reason than because I had loved the football team ever since I was old enough to remember and I had always known OU was where I was going to go. As with everything else in my life up to that point, I was unable to see anything bigger or further out than what was right in front of me, which was a state school. Never for a second did I consider applying to or attending a school out of state. It was as if I didn't even know that leaving the state of Oklahoma was an option.

OU is a great school that provided a great education and plenty of opportunities and I loved my time there, but I definitely gave no consideration about the quality of the education it provided or what I might want to study at OU or any other school. I don't recommend the football team as a reason for choosing a school, but at that point in my life, I wasn't really into analyzing my opportunities or choices. I secured a dorm assignment as well as a roommate, who was a high school buddy of mine. I was all set to go with my financial aid with one little catch: I needed a cosigner for the loans that had been awarded.

As I quickly learned, a cosigner is somebody who agrees to take on the responsibility of paying back a debt if the person the loan was intended for fails to repay the debt themselves. Since I was not yet eighteen years old at the time that the financial aid forms had to be signed, I needed a cosigner.

So I asked my mother. She said no. I begged; I pleaded. She still said no. She explained how she could not take the risk and put herself in that situation if something went wrong and I dropped out or defaulted on my loan payments. She still had three kids at home and could not afford that extra financial burden.

And honestly, who could blame her? What had I done to prove to anyone that I could be financially responsible enough to be trusted to manage money in such a way that I would be able to pay back the loans?

I had failed. I wouldn't be attending OU or any college for the time being. Not because I hadn't thought big enough, but because I hadn't executed on the small things. I didn't plan. I didn't prepare. I had somehow thought that college was just going to magically happen on its own. And when I finally did come up with a plan, it was the wrong plan for me.

Today is a different story. I still dream big, but I execute small. I have all kinds of goals. In fact, I keep a list of them! I have financial goals, professional goals, travel goals, health goals, learning goals, family goals, and goals I just put into a miscellaneous category.

I can't possibly get to them all at once, but when I choose one, I set my sights on it. I think it through from start to finish and set a series of small steps that will help me achieve the goal in the best way possible. Sure, things never go perfectly as planned, but I've learned that if I do the proper due diligence from the beginning, I usually don't have to alter my steps or plan too much.

An example is the health goal I have set for myself to remain under 200 pounds. There are several reasons for this goal: I don't like to spend money on new clothes because I've outgrown them, I don't like to spend money on medical bills, and I want to remain as physically active as possible for my family so that I can continue playing with my children, coaching their sports teams, and just being a good example for them.

So, I've set short-term goals to support my long-term goal.

Goals like exercising four to five days a week, training for and running a 5K with each of my children when they reach the age to do so, and running a 5K in my fifties and sixties (I'm forty-five today). I explore and try different healthy eating alternatives. When I get tired or bored with one, I move on to another. And I'll continue to set new short-term goals as I go, with the ultimate goal of staying fit, in shape, and as healthy as I can be.

Without short-term goals, the chances of achieving my long-term goals decrease significantly. I would be basically just floating along, hoping it happens without taking control and *making* it happen. That is exactly what happened with my big-picture goal of going to college—I just floated along, out of control and financially hoping that college would happen when I wanted it to. Guess what? It didn't.

Maybe your goal isn't college. Maybe it's to enlist in the military. My 19-year-old stepson decided college wasn't for him and he wasn't excited about any options he had in the workforce, so he enlisted in the Air Force.

In doing your research and talking to recruiters, you determine a particular job you want in the military and set that as your goal. Because the military does its best to match jobs with appropriate personnel, you buy the study materials to best prepare in advance for the ASVAB test in the hopes that you will achieve a high enough score to qualify for the job you want. You set daily study goals to improve your scores for each subsequent practice test that you take leading up to the real test day. Once enlisted, you focus on preparing for basic training. You find out what the requirements are to complete the basic training physical fitness test. How many push-ups and sit-ups do you have to do in the allotted time and how quickly do you have to complete the running test? Maybe you want to be in great shape ahead of boot camp and be able to pass the test before even leaving, so you begin training at home with specific goals to improve your fitness levels each month in the lead-up to leaving. To accomplish your monthly goals, you set weekly goals for improvement. Getting the idea?

Maybe you want to buy a car as soon as you can after turning sixteen. Your first goal is getting a job. Then you set up separate savings accounts, one for the car itself and one for insurance and maintenance. You have 50% of each paycheck auto deposited to your car savings and 20% auto deposited to your insurance savings so that you can pay for your first six months and following payments once you buy the car. The last 30% goes to your other wants, like entertainment and dining.

No matter the goal, figure out the smaller goals you need to achieve first and in what order so that you can successfully accomplish the big goal. Write it down. Start with the big goal in mind and set a deadline for it. Then begin working backward to determine each of the smaller supporting goals and the deadlines to achieve *those* goals in order to achieve the big goal by its deadline. You will set many big goals and dreams in life, but the only way to get there is to execute the small steps first!

6

Impulse Buying

"I love money. I love everything about it. I bought some pretty good stuff. Got me a $300 pair of socks. Got a fur sink. An electric dog polisher. A gasoline-powered turtleneck sweater. And, of course, I bought some dumb stuff, too."
— **Steve Martin,** American actor, comedian, writer, and musician

Without a doubt, the single worst habit I developed was impulse buying. It turned out to be a habit that would haunt me for nearly two decades and one that a huge part of our society is dealing with today.

According to recent studies and surveys, impulse buying is a bigger problem than it's ever been. The percentage of us who admit to impulse buying continues to rise, and it's usually money spent on ourselves. According to a study commissioned by Finder in July of 2017 (their mission is to assist people in making better financial decisions), 64% of those surveyed admitted to making an impulse purchase at least once a month, and nearly 45% said that they experienced feelings of regret afterward. While impulse buying is most likely to take place on the spot in a store, with the rise in online shopping via phones, tablets, and computers, it has become increasingly easier to impulse buy from anywhere.

The problem with impulse buying is we don't slow down or take the time to think about the purchase itself. We don't plan the purchase or give any thought to the long-term effects of the purchase on any other aspect of our lives or on our financial well-being.

We don't ask ourselves if the item in question is something we truly want or need. What are the potential additional costs associated with the purchase, such as warranties, upgrades, maintenance, storage, and disposal? What effect is the purchase going to have on our short- and long-term goals? For example, saving for a phone (short-term) or saving for a car (long-term).

Your best chance of preventing impulse buying from developing into a bad habit and wreaking havoc on your life is to learn how to distinguish between a want and a need as early as possible. "Needs" are things like food, water, shelter, clothing, transportation, and basic hygiene and personal care products, i.e., things that are most likely provided by your parents or other adults in your life. "Wants" are things like a new car, phone, television, and video games.

It's also important to distinguish between needs and wants within the "needs" category. For example, you don't need to overspend on name-brand clothing, like the Guess jeans and Ralph Lauren Polo shirts I desired. Non-label clothing works just as well.

Every time you hear yourself say you "need" something, check yourself. I do this not only for myself, but also for everyone else in my family. If I hear my teenage stepson say he needs more data for his phone, I'll say, "Do you *need* more data, or do you *want* more data?"

You probably need transportation (most of us do), but *how much* transportation you need should be the focus. Do you really need a car, or can you make do with public transportation? Can you walk or ride a bike? If these other means of transportation truly do not work for your situation, than your choice of car should be focused on affordability and reliability. You don't need a Mustang or Camaro to drive to your shift at McDonald's or Walmart.

What about food? Of course we all need food, but do we need to eat out every night of the week or even three times a week? There was a stretch of several years when my family and I were spending $600 to $800 per month eating out. Rarely was it ever planned. It was usually just an impulse decision.

On the low end of $600 per month, that totaled $7,200 per year. Annually, $10,000 of my pre-tax wages were needed to fund this $7,200-a-year food habit. That meant working roughly 285 hours per year to simply eat out. Think about that for a moment. At 40 hours per work week, that equals slightly more than seven weeks of work per year.

For someone making $15 per hour, such as a teenager or a college student, spending $10 per day eating out comes to approximately $4,200 a year in pre-tax wages. That would equate to roughly 280 hours, almost the same amount of time I was spending at work.

Now think about how happy you are at work or how much

you enjoy your job. Statistics show that about half of us are satisfied overall with our jobs, which means that half of us are going to jobs we don't like or are not satisfied with in order to support habits and impulse purchases like the ones I just described.

That's what I was doing. Because I was unhappy in certain areas of my life, I was trying to find happiness through constantly buying things I thought I wanted or by finding a temporary escape by spending an hour at a restaurant. What I finally discovered, though, was that if I stopped focusing so much on things I thought I wanted and focused more on supporting my actual needs, I wouldn't require nearly the amount of income I was earning.

If we prepared less-expensive but more-satisfying food at home, found less-expensive or free entertainment options, paid off our vehicles and kept them instead of replacing them with newer ones—and thus new car payments—then I could find a fulfilling job I really wanted to do, even if it paid less. A *lot* less. And that's what I've done.

I came to this realization simply by figuring out what was really a "need" and what was a "want." I discovered my true wants were not the things I was always impulsively buying. My true *want* was the financial freedom to do what truly makes me happy and doing the work I want to do, which in part is writing this book.

It's fine to want things and have things we want, but we must know the difference between a "need" and a "want" so that we can make sound financial decisions. The key is to be honest about it. Don't talk yourself into something being a *need* because you *want* it so badly.

If you discover there is something you want, don't just

immediately buy it. Take some time to think about it. How much will you use it? How much joy or satisfaction will you get out of it? What will you do with it if you decide you no longer want it?

Whether it's a less expensive item (short-term) or a more expensive item (long-term), make it a goal and save for it. Then when you have enough money for it, think about it some more and decide if it is something worth your hard-earned savings. By working through this process, you may find that it is something you don't want after all.

One exercise really brought home to me the negative effects of impulse buying. I got the idea of it during the first year I was home after I had left corporate America. I had considered creating a podcast, and during my research, I came across the duo called "The Minimalists," made up of Joshua Fields Millburn and Ryan Nicodemus. I wasn't yet familiar with minimalism, but I was intrigued by both their message and the simplicity with which they delivered it. Based on this new-to-me concept of minimalism, I went through our entire house looking for things that we never used or hardly ever used.

My goal was to purge our home of all the things we didn't need or no longer wanted no matter how much we had spent on a particular item when we bought it. I gave no thought to possibly using an item later. If I found an item my wife and I had bought five years ago and had only used once, we were not going to hold on to it "just in case" we might use it one more time in the next five years. It was gone. I went through closets, drawers, the garage, the attic—everywhere!—and donated all of the items.

When I share this with others, I am inevitably asked why I chose to donate instead of sell the items. When I was younger (before I had a family and kids), I likely would have taken the time to attempt to sell the items. I used to do the whole eBay exercise of selling and shipping, having the occasional garage sale, taking things to consignment stores, etc. But these days, free time is in shorter supply, and I decided to trade the pennies on the dollar I would have likely recouped for the time I saved by donating. My time was too valuable to spend.

I'm also asked if I think about all the money we had spent on the things we gave away. The answer is yes. I think about all the hours I spent at jobs I didn't like. I think about the cost of storing and moving the items. I think about the experiences we missed out on because of the money we spent on those possessions. And I also think about the time spent buying, cleaning, and getting rid of the items. Those are the regrets I have: that we bought the items to begin with, not that we ended up giving them away.

That process turned out to be a profound lesson about the reality of our impulsive and bad purchases. Thousands of dollars spent on things we thought we wanted but never needed. Purchases we obviously didn't take the time to think through. And there is *not one thing* we have regretted giving away. Not once have we said we wished we had something back. And we have never gone out and repurchased an item we gave away.

Looking back on when I was a teenager, I honestly don't know why I was spending all of my money on baseball cards. The only thing I can think of is that at the time they were something I wanted. They certainly weren't anything I needed. They were going to sit boxed in a closet until someday when I needed or wanted the money from selling them, which I hoped would be later in life after they had increased in value.

I loved sports and looked up to professional athletes and I

enjoyed the time I spent with friends collecting, but what was the end game? How long would I collect? How much money was I willing to spend on them? What goals was I willing to sacrifice? What other goals might that money have helped me reach? I had no idea and gave it no thought.

And I certainly didn't give any thought to the additional costs associated with collecting. I had to buy boxes to store the less-valuable cards in. I had to buy pocketed sheets and three-ring binders to showcase the cards that personally meant something to me. And I had to buy more durable protective cases to keep the more valuable cards safe and protect their value. I must have spent thousands of dollars alone on the supplies necessary to collect, but I gave those items no consideration when I first began buying cards. While this additional cost wouldn't have prevented me from collecting, if I had thought about it, it may have provided me with some boundaries in terms of the amount of money I was going to spend on buying cards.

When we're young, how many of us give consideration to the true cost of ownership when it comes to buying our first vehicle? The routine maintenance such as changing the oil, air filter, or spark plugs? The everyday cost of fuel? Will the car require regular gasoline or premium and how many miles per gallon will the car travel? What about insurance? Will you buy a car that will only require liability coverage, or will full coverage be required? Does the type of car you want cost more to insure than another? What about tires? How much do they cost for a set and how often will they need to be replaced? I live in a part of the country where pickup trucks are everywhere, including in high school parking lots. How much do those big tires cost to replace, even if just one from a blowout or a nail?

When you have determined that there is something you need

or want, make a list of all of the additional costs associated with the purchase and estimate what those costs will be. Maybe you decide that you want to upgrade from the basic phone you currently have that simply allows you to call and text to a new smartphone. You have determined which brand and model you can comfortably afford and a minimal data plan to go with it, because you're going to get Wi-Fi set up at home or go to a coffee shop and use the "free" Wi-Fi there.

Now, I know what you are thinking. Why would you have to set up Wi-Fi at home? It's already there and your parents pay for it. Well, I know people who don't have Wi-Fi. And I know that if I didn't have Wi-Fi and my teen or young adult child still living at home came to me wanting Wi-Fi for entertainment purposes that I didn't need myself, I sure wouldn't be the one paying for it.

So if you decide to pay for it yourself, how much is installation going to cost? How much is the monthly fee? How much will a maintenance call cost if you have to call a tech out to repair something? When you go to the coffee shop to use their Wi-Fi, what is that going to cost you? How far away is it from home? How much is the gas going to cost for the round trip? How much is a cup of coffee going to cost you while you are there?

What if your original data plan doesn't cut it and you need to upgrade to a more suitable plan each month or you just need to buy some additional data every once in a while? What is that going to cost? What about a protective case and a protection warranty at the time of purchase? An extended warranty when the original one expires? What about apps, games, music, earbuds, or headphones?

Don't guess on these potential additional costs. Research and spend the time to get the real numbers. Most information is easily attainable these days if you just put in the time to find it. If you are considering a plan with 2GB of data, simply typing "how much is 2GB of data" into a Google search reveals estimates for Internet browsing, how much time can be spent streaming audio or video, how many emails can be sent, how many photos can be uploaded to social media, and so forth.

Don't take shortcuts and don't guess! If you guess, you will always guess low. Why? Because you really want the item in question and you want the numbers to work to justify the purchase.

If it is an item you simply want and don't need, this process will help you determine how badly you really want it, because you'll have to determine how much you are willing to spend on taking care of it, maintaining it, and getting the most out of it. If it is an item you need, this process will help you determine what you can afford to buy based on how much you can afford to spend on taking care of it and maintaining it.

When it comes to impulse buying, it's the small things that really get us. It's the small things that add up, because we don't have any real knowledge of how much we are actually spending.

When I speak to teenagers or young adults about impulse buying, the number-one thing mentioned is food. In fact, when I'm in a high school classroom giving a presentation, nearly every single student will walk in with a drink or some kind of junk food they've just purchased at the school snack shop.

Avoid the temptation to impulsively buy. Take a different route. Don't visit online shopping sites that make it easier to impulsively buy than actually getting up and going out to get something. Avoid shopping areas like malls. Make a list of the things you really need and don't buy anything not on it. The point is, the opportunity to impulsively buy things we don't necessarily need is *everywhere*. And if we don't learn early on to slow down, think about what we are purchasing, and consider what impact it will have on our goals and other areas of our lives, we are creating a terrible habit that will set us up for tough times for years to come.

By "tough times," I mean not having enough to take care of basic needs such as shelter, transportation, and health. Maybe you have to move back in with your parents because you can no longer afford suitable housing. Maybe you take risks, like driving on worn-out tires because you can't afford new ones. Maybe you don't go to the doctor when you really should. Maybe you have to put off or give up on a goal, such as going to college or trade school, like I did.

Not too long ago, my 19-year-old stepson asked if he could move in with us. On his 18th birthday during his senior year of high school, he had decided he was ready to be on his own, said a few choice words to his father, and moved out of his house. Even though he had been working for a while, my stepson was not financially prepared to be on his own because he had not set any goals leading up to the day and had impulsively blown through all of his earnings.

Prior to him asking us if he could move in with us, we had learned that while he was couch surfing from one place to another, he had let his auto insurance lapse. Not only that, he no longer had medical insurance because he had chosen not to set aside money to pay for it. We had already explained to him the risks associated with not having insurance and had gone over all of the what-ifs.

Still, instead of parking his car and setting aside money for an insurance policy, he had continued to drive while also continuing to spend his earnings on other things. By the time he came to us for a place to stay, he had been an uninsured motorist for around three months.

We agreed to let him stay with us, but only if he continued to work and get car insurance. He'd have to make changes to his spending habits in order to make paying for auto insurance a priority. We also agreed that in order to help him with that insurance, we would let him buy insurance through our policy so that it would be more affordable for him.

About three months after he became insured, he was involved in an auto accident on a highway. His vehicle was totaled and he took an ambulance ride to an emergency room, where he was examined and underwent X-rays. The other driver's vehicle sustained considerable damage. While my stepson was fortunate to not be ticketed, he was found to be at fault by the insurance companies. The total cost associated with the accident was more than $10,000.

What if this had happened three months earlier when he wasn't insured? He wouldn't have had the money to pay for anything he was liable for. He couldn't have paid the towing bill for his vehicle and the $20-per-day fee he was being charged for it to sit at the tow yard. He couldn't have paid the bills that resulted from the ambulance ride and emergency room visit, which could have easily ended up in collections (resulting in damaged credit). He couldn't have paid for the other driver's vehicle repairs, which may have ended up in a lawsuit that entailed additional costs such as attorney fees.

For three months, he put himself at this great risk simply because he chose to impulsively spend his money on wants instead of responsibly focusing on his needs.

One fall while I was at the University of Oklahoma, it was a home-football-game Saturday. I was twenty-four or twenty-five years old at the time and still working on my undergraduate degree because I had gotten such a late start due to my poor financial habits. As on any game weekend, I was walking around with friends, enjoying the pregame atmosphere prior to going into the stadium for the game.

As I was walking through the area known as "campus corner," I came across someone selling tickets to an upcoming game. It wasn't just any game—he was selling a pair of tickets to the Oklahoma–Texas game a couple of weeks away. That was *the* game! It's played in Dallas every year because Dallas is approximately halfway between the two campuses. Half of the tickets are allotted for Texas fans; the other half go to Oklahoma fans. I had been once before, two years earlier, and Oklahoma had lost. I was anxious to go back and hopefully experience a different outcome.

I asked the guy how much for the two tickets. He said $150 each, $300 for the pair. Without hesitation, I said to him, "Wait right here! I'll be right back." I raced as fast as I could to the nearest convenience store to find an ATM machine and withdrew the $300 in cash. I ran back to the corner where the guy was standing and handed him the $300. The tickets were mine.

In this moment of extreme impulsiveness, I had failed to consider anything else that a game and a trip like this would require. The cost of gas to drive to Dallas and back. The cost of a hotel room for Friday and Saturday night since I wanted to enjoy the full experience of the game and everything that came with it on game day. The cost of parking at the hotel and at the game. The cost of food and drink for the weekend. The lost income from taking the entire weekend off from my job, which was the part of the week when I made most of my money.

How was this single moment of impulsive buying going to impact my goals of paying my apartment rent, paying the utilities, buying groceries, and buying everything else I actually needed? What about ensuring that I would have enough money to pay for my tuition and books the following semester?

The answer is "Negative." My single moment of failing to think about my future was going to have a massive negative impact on everything. That's exactly what impulse buying does—when we don't give proper consideration to our purchases, we can put all of our priorities and goals in jeopardy. And if we make it a habit the way I did, it can be extremely difficult to break the habit even as it's negatively impacting nearly every other aspect of our well-being.

I could go on and on about the dangers of impulse buying, how difficult the habit is to break once started, and the importance of understanding the difference between wants and needs to combat it, but no matter what I say, some people just enjoy shopping and buying. They love the thrill of the hunt, going to the mall with friends, the adrenaline rush of finding a great deal too good to pass up.

For some, it's just a different form of entertainment. I learned this when one time I questioned someone close to me regarding their habit of shopping and they politely explained that for them, shopping was no different than me choosing to spend my money on going to a sporting event or concert. My response to that is, "Yes, I can see that reasoning. Just be sure that you set boundaries to protect yourself from overspending." And also include a set amount of money you can afford to spend on shopping in your entertainment budget. We'll talk about that more later.

By setting boundaries, you can still enjoy all of the emotions and feelings that come with shopping, but at the same time you've planned for it and you've set limits that will reduce the risk of neglecting or sacrificing your needs for your impulsivity and wants.

7

Beware of Credit Cards

"When I was young, people lived from paycheck to paycheck. Today, it seems like they live from credit card payment to credit card payment."
— **Robert Kiyosaki**, Best-selling author of the *Rich Dad Poor Dad* series

I cannot state this strongly enough: beware of credit cards! This is not some standard warning that I'm throwing out there. It's a warning from someone who has had problems with credit cards. As you're about to find out, I had *huge* problems, problems that almost derailed all of my plans.

I know what you're thinking: *If everyone has credit cards, then what's the big deal? What problems did you have that were so bad? You get one, use it, and pay it off on time each month. What can go wrong?* Trust me, a lot can go wrong.

You are eligible for a credit card the second you turn eighteen.

But are you *ready* for a credit card? Are you mature enough to use it in a responsible manner? Not sure? Do a quick review of your short time as a money manager, which for most of you is likely only a few years.

How well have you done controlling your impulse buying? Do you truly understand the difference between "wants" and "needs"? What saving habits have you developed? Have you borrowed money from family, friends, or coworkers and had problems paying it back in a timely manner or at all? Do you keep track of your expenditures using an online money management tool? Do you use a transaction register for your debit card purchases?

These are all key indicators that will provide valuable insight as to whether or not you are ready to be a responsible credit card holder. If I had taken the time to do this simple, brief evaluation, the answer would have been easy: No. I was clearly not financially responsible enough or ready to have a credit card in any way.

My dream of going away to attend a big, four-year state college had been squashed as I was nearing my high school graduation. I graduated in May of 1993 and had given up my paper route and my job at Pizza Hut. Shortly after graduation, I landed my next gig as a deep-fry cook at Long John Silver's. I know—sweet job, right? To make the deal even sweeter, I agreed to close the kitchen Sunday through Thursday in exchange for having every Friday and Saturday off.

I'd fry food from 4:00 pm until around 9:00 pm, getting splattered by hot oil that would blister my hands and end up in scars. The other cooks and I would get burned so badly at times that the customers in the lobby would hear the occasional four-letter obscenity from the back.

Around 9:00 pm each night, I would fry up one last oversized batch of food so we could get started on our closing duties early. I could start cleaning the oil and the rest of the kitchen without being interrupted by having to cook. I learned that by doing this, I could usually get out of there an hour after close (around 11:00 pm) instead of sometime between midnight and 1:00 am. Plus, since I had cooked up a bunch of food, there was usually a little extra for "someone" to take home.

At that point, I was making more money than I ever had. Was I saving any of it? Come on! Of course not. Did I have anything of value to show for it? Not really. I was no longer collecting sports cards, but I was still finding a way to blow money as quickly as I could earn it.

I knew I still wanted to go to college, and by then I had come to terms with the fact that the only way it was going to happen was if I paid for it myself. So what did I do? Eyes on the goal, right? Figure out the small goals and create the plan, right? Not me! I opened one of the credit card offers I was receiving daily in the mail and applied for a credit card. Instead of creating a plan and the baby steps that would allow me to save money and get to college, I was searching for ways to get access to more money that I could spend.

It seemed like I was receiving a new credit card offer every day. Even though I was making more money than I ever had and spending it on more junk that I had ever thought I wanted, it wasn't enough. There was no desire or even a thought to save. It was get more, spend more, by any means possible.

What I failed to understand about credit cards was that the only real value they provide at such a young age is being a useful tool to begin to build up a good credit score. If you apply for a credit card at such a young age for any reason other than that, you are simply asking for trouble.

Why do you need a good credit score? A good credit score shows a lender such as a bank that when you apply for a mortgage loan to buy a home or for a loan to buy a new car, you are trustworthy and likely to repay the loan according to the terms stipulated.

How do you responsibly build a good credit score? By using the credit card very sparingly for *only* the things you need. Maybe you decide you're going to only put gas for your vehicle on your credit card each month. Then the bill arrives in the mail, and you pay the full amount owed on time. By repeatedly doing this, you are showing lenders that you can make a payment by the due date. You will also have avoided the late payment penalty fees and interest charges that occur when you carry a balance forward into the following months.

Unless you plan to have a couple hundred thousand dollars in cash saved up to pay for a home, you will likely need to take out a loan to buy it. And in order to get a loan with reasonable terms (like a low interest rate) or any kind of loan at all, you will need to have a good credit score. I understand that some people say that credit cards are not needed for anything and that you should never get one, but in my opinion, that is just not realistic. But again, beware and only get one if you are mature enough in your financial journey to handle the responsibility of having one.

A few weeks after I mailed my application in, I received my first credit card in the mail. By then, I was approaching my nineteenth birthday and had moved on to a job at a Hallmark shop in our local mall. I was walking or riding a bike the three miles to the mall and back home each day.

I didn't use the card too much in the beginning. I was even

able to pay it off as I went! So I was building decent credit. But then I came up with a great idea: if I used the credit card to buy the junk I wanted—fast food, clothes, CDs, etc.—then I could use the cash I was making from work to pay for classes and books at the Rogers State College branch in Bartlesville.

Rogers State College was a four-year public school in Claremore, Oklahoma with a couple of branches around the state so that those who didn't live in Claremore could attend. Now it's Rogers State University or RSU. We also had a private school, Bartlesville Wesleyan College, now called Oklahoma Wesleyan University. Being a private school, I assumed it was much more expensive and out of my price range, so I never looked into it.

So, Rogers State College it was! In the fall of 1994, I enrolled in a couple of basic classes and paid cash for them and the books I needed. I was finally a college student, only not the one I had hoped to be—I was still living at home and taking classes in the evenings in the small classrooms at the Rogers State enrollment building or in a room at my old high school.

As I began to take classes, I followed through on my plan and began to use my credit card more, buying clothes, shoes, CDs, fast food, etc. And since I was spending the money I earned from my job to pay for my classes and books, I was only making the minimum payment each month on my credit card.

Because I wasn't paying off the full balance each month, I was being charged interest. You may be curious how interest is actually calculated and how it affects what you *really* end up paying for things. When you get a credit card, it comes with what is called an annual percentage rate or an APR. The average credit card interest rate for new offers during the fourth quarter of 2019 was 19.02% according to WalletHub's Credit Card Landscape Report. The average interest rate of all credit card accounts between 1991 and early 2020 ranged between just below 12% to nearly 19% according to WalletHub. Credit card interest rates are always high and can be very costly.

Let's say you apply for a card and are approved for a $2,000 credit limit. You decide to buy some stuff and rack up $1,500 in debt by the end of the first month. You can't make the full payment, so you decide to just pay the minimum. If your balance is over $1,000, the minimum payment due will be a percentage of the balance, usually around 2%. If you owe less than $1,000, it is typically a fixed fee, usually in the range of $25. But different cards have different policies for these amounts.

By not making the full payment, you trigger the interest penalty. To calculate the interest, you begin by converting the annual percentage rate to a daily percentage rate. You do that by dividing the interest rate by 365, the number of days in a year. In this example, the daily interest rate would be 19.02/365, which equals .05%. Doesn't seem bad, does it? Keep reading.

Next, you calculate the average daily balance for the month in question. The average daily balance will increase with purchases and decrease when you make a payment. Starting with your beginning balance on the first day, add up the balances for each day of the month. Since you just got your card and started off with a $0 balance at the beginning and grew the balance to $1,500 by the end of the month, let's say the average daily balance was $700.

Next, multiply the average daily balance by the daily interest rate. Here we have $700 multiplied by .05%, which is .35. Finally, we multiply that number by the days in the billing cycle and get an interest amount of $10.50.

Seems pretty harmless, right? Just $10.50—no big deal. But now look what happens. Remember, you only made the minimum payment, which in this example would be $1,500 multiplied by 2%, which is $30. So on the first day of the next billing cycle, you now you have a balance of $1,480.50: $1,470 in purchases carried over plus the $10.50 in interest.

You make some more minor purchases, maybe $150 worth since you don't have a lot left before you're maxed out. But because you carried over your balance from last month, your average daily balance is now $1,500. Using the same formula we used before, your interest charge is now $23.25.

And the worst part is that *you are paying interest on your interest*. Remember that $10.50 in interest from last month? That's right! Part of the $23.25 you were just charged was interest for not paying that off.

Now imagine that you've maxed out your credit card. Since you have no more credit, you are blowing all of your earnings on junk to the point that you can't even make the minimum payment on time. You incur late fees for late payments. Your interest keeps increasing each month because the minimum payment you get around to paying after the due date isn't enough to lower your average daily balance, which actually keeps rising each month.

With all of the purchases, interest, and late fees, you are actually carrying over a balance higher than the $2,000 credit limit. Guess what? A penalty or fee for being over your credit limit is tacked on. Now the late payments and being over your credit limit triggers an interest rate increase from 19% to 30% and the cycle continues month after month until this behavior changes and you pay down the debt.

Do this for a year or three as I did, and do you know how much extra in interest and fees you end up paying for that convenience store junk food, that Starbucks coffee, and those games you bought on your phone? In this example, with a few late payments and over-limit fees added on plus the increase in the interest rate, the added cost for the first year alone would exceed $500.

Imagine using a credit card to buy something on sale with the thought that you are saving money…only to actually not save anything at all or spend even more than the item was initially worth. Imagine paying an extra $500 (or more) for, say, $1,800 worth of stuff. Stuff you didn't need. And that's just one year. Imagine letting the debt go on without making a dent in paying it off for multiple years. That $500 becomes thousands of dollars. Finally, imagine that you haven't done this with a small $2,000 credit limit, but with a $10,000 limit. A credit limit *five times* the size of this example. Lucky for me, I didn't have access to that much credit at the time, but there are many who do. And who knows what would have happened to me if I did?

Don't think this can happen to you? I promise you, it can. On top of all of the financial problems it caused me, it was negatively affecting my credit score that I would need someday. (And that you'll need, too.) I was showing potential lenders that I couldn't handle the responsibility of credit and borrowing money. I couldn't be trusted to pay it back in accordance with the agreed-upon terms. In other words, I was a risk. And when you become a financial risk, you pay for it—literally—in the form of fewer options and poor terms such as high interest rates.

That's not just limited to credit cards, either. It includes any type of loan you may want from a bank or any other lender, including car loans, personal student loans, or a mortgage for a house. While some of you very likely may never plan to own a home and will prefer to rent instead, even rental companies and landlords check credit history. And when they do find a rental applicant with a bad credit score and poor credit history, what do they do? They reject them or charge more up front to get into the apartment, duplex, condo, house, etc. Instead of first month's rent and a minor deposit for cleaning and repairs when you vacate the property, it may be first month's rent, last month's rent, and a security deposit for cleaning and damages equal to another month's rent. Next thing you know, an apartment that would have cost you $750 to get into with good credit ends up costing you $1,500 just to get the keys to the place.

Now that you have an understanding of the dangers of credit card debt, allow me to return to my story. I continued taking classes, but not consistently because I didn't always have the money to pay the tuition. In my poorly-thought-out scheme, I had never considered that I would actually max out my credit cards, but that is exactly what happened. I managed to use up the entire credit line and could no longer make any more purchases with my card. Since I had no more credit, I began using up most of my income to buy junk while only leaving enough to make the minimum payment on my credit card. In doing this, I no longer had anything to use to consistently pay for additional classes.

So, I just took classes when I could. It was one semester on, one off. Three hours here or six hours there because I could only afford a class or two at a time instead of going full-time like I should have been. At that rate, I'd be lucky to graduate by the time I was thirty.

In the meantime, I took a second part-time job at the mall at a baseball card shop. At that time, it was a dream job compared to anything I had done previously. No manual labor like mowing lawns, no getting up early like I did when delivering newspapers, and no fast food. I got to sit around and talk to people about sports and collecting. While I hadn't collected in a couple of years, I was still a sports enthusiast and had never completely lost interest in it.

Eventually, I quit the Hallmark store when the baseball card shop became a full-time deal. I worked forty-plus hours a week, sometimes eleven-hour days from open to close, sometimes just a few hours in the evening.

It was as cushy as it gets, yet sometimes very boring. Card collecting is a niche hobby and usually made up of a small community of collectors. So much so that there would be days when there might only be a visitor or two and the shop would do no sales. You can imagine how long and boring those days could be.

After a few short months of avoiding the temptation, to pass the time, I began to open packs of cards. Not because I was collecting like I did when I was a kid, but because I was now bored and gambling. I was gambling on the fact that I would hit the big card. The one I could sell to an actual collector and make some money on.

I paid for the cards on payday when my debt was deducted directly from my paycheck. I'd keep a running tab each week of the packs of cards I'd opened and on payday I would report it to my boss, who would subtract the amount owed from my check. And more often than not, I would walk out without a paycheck at all and only a box of cards in my hand. I carried on this way for three years.

I would occasionally hit the big card and get a little payback, but as with any sort of gambling, it usually didn't satisfy me and end there—I'd keep trying to do it again and again. And usually I'd end up in such a hole that no matter the payoff, I was always behind.

To make things worse, I had gotten sucked into something new: I started gambling on sports contests. I'd gamble on football and basketball games, both college and pro. I'd even bet on baseball and occasionally horse racing.

Things like this are not uncommon when we make bad choices. Something that seems pretty harmless in the beginning (like some poor decisions with money when you are fifteen or sixteen) can set the tone for years to come. It can lead you down a path that you are never able to get off of. In my case, the horrible financial habits I had acquired became a gateway to something even worse. I'm not sure if I ever became a gambling addict, but I was walking that line.

At the end of 1997, I was twenty-two years old and still wanted to go to college. But my terrible money habits that had begun nearly ten years earlier had progressed to other negative habits and had become so bad and out of control that it was looking like college was never going to happen. Instead, I was drowning in credit card debt and gambling and was working for baseball cards. At my lowest point, I was $4,500 in debt and had more than 100,000 baseball cards. I was still living at home and still had no money.

I know it may seem strange that I was living at home this entire time, yet this was possible. Once I got older, my mom and dad were very hands-off parents, which I appreciated. I worked all through high school, had decent grades—slightly above a 3.0 until my final semester, when senioritis kicked in—and had never had any discipline issues or been in trouble with the law.

Pretty much from the time I was eighteen, that was my life given that I continued to satisfy my mom's requirement: as long as I was either working or going to school, I was allowed to stay at home rent-free. I was always doing one of those; some of the time, I was doing both.

The truth is, I don't recall that anyone ever knew or seriously questioned me about my situation. And I sure wasn't going to share with anyone what I was doing! I wasn't about to tell my parents how much debt I was in or that I was spending all of my money on sports cards or that I was gambling. All of that was too embarrassing to share. While I felt some minor embarrassment about still living at home at twenty-two, never once having gotten out on my own, there was nothing I could do about it given my choices with money. If anyone did ask me in passing or during small talk about what my plans were for moving out, going to college, or anything along those lines, I would just say I was getting closer, still working out the details, or hadn't decided for sure yet between whatever options I pretended to have.

"What about the cards piling up?" you might be asking yourself. Someone had to notice that, right? Well, they were in a locked closet. I had replaced the regular doorknob with a locking one that would keep anyone without a key out of it. When I came home with a box of cards, I'd go straight to the closet, unlock it, put the box in, and lock the door. It was known that cards were there, but nobody knew how high the stacks of boxes had gotten or just how full the closet had become. And since I had taken some college classes off and on that neither of my parents had paid for, the logical conclusion was that I was spending my hard-earned income on college classes.

I certainly don't fault my parents or question why they never intervened. It was obvious that I didn't want that by the lengths I went to cover things up. And even if they had, I'm not sure how effective it would have been.

In early 1998, as I was approaching my twenty-third birthday, I decided enough was enough. It was now or never for me to get my act together and go away to college. One of my brothers was a year younger than me and was moving closer and closer toward his college graduation, and my youngest brother had recently moved away to join him at the University of Arkansas.

I finally devised a plan that made sense: I would stop buying baseball cards, sell what I could of the 100,000 cards I had accumulated to help pay off my debt, cut up my credit cards, save up some money, and move away to college. If I did that now, combined with the forty-five hours of college credit I had accumulated, I might be able to get through college before I was thirty.

As I was waiting for my acceptance letter from the University of Oklahoma to arrive, I met with as many card shop owners and collectors as I could to sell as many cards as possible. I finally sold enough to pay off my credit card debt. The bad part was that I sold my cards for pennies on the dollar compared to what I had paid for them and what they were supposedly worth. But nevertheless, I was out of debt.

I managed to save up almost $3,000 dollars in just a few months. It's amazing how quickly you can amass savings when you make it an intentional goal and cut out the impulsive spending! With that money, I bought a 1983 Honda Accord from my dad for $850 dollars, went to Norman, Oklahoma, and put down my deposit and first month's rent on an apartment.

I had applied for financial aid and had received enough to pay for my tuition and books. The time had finally come! I had a clean slate and was finally doing what I had always imagined myself doing, just much later.

8

Be Careful with Student Loans

"Some debts are fun when you are acquiring them, but none are fun when you set about retiring them."
— **Ogden Nash**, Poet

By the middle of August of 1998, I finally moved away from home for the first time. Because I was twenty-two years old when I applied for financial aid this time around, I no longer had to list my mother as a provider and list her income on the application. I also did not need a cosigner since I was now of legal age. The loans were mine, all mine. I was the only one responsible for paying them back.

Since only my income was considered and there was very little of it, I was awarded both loans and grants. The grants I received were a specific amount based on need and they were not required to be paid back.

Between this money and the cash I still had remaining after

my initial expenses, I figured I'd be able to move and go to school without having to work. I could go to class, go to the gym, go out and have some fun, and do a little studying. I figured that each semester when my new financial aid loans and grants came in, there would be enough to sustain my schooling as well as my living expenses as long as I did not squander the money. What part of my track record in personal finance made me think I would *not* squander the money is beyond me.

There was one other thing I hadn't considered or had even known would be a problem, although it probably should have been pretty obvious. In the beginning, I was on the high of living my dream. But as time went by—and it didn't take long—I began to realize more and more that I was by myself. I had no family or friends around and I was not the outgoing type who easily talked to people I didn't know, not even if they were sitting right next to me in a classroom.

I pretty much kept to myself. In the classroom, I only talked to people if the work required it. At the gym, the extent of my talking to anyone consisted of asking for an occasional spot. And at the time, I wasn't really the kind of person to go out anywhere by myself where I might meet people. After going to classes in the mornings and afternoons and spending a short time studying, in the evenings I spent most of my time calling friends and family.

At that time, there were no cell phones. When you made a long-distance phone call from your land line, you were charged by the minute. A long-distance call was anything outside of the defined local calling area. Whether it was within the local area code made no difference—if you were calling a neighboring town, the next state over, or across the country, if it was outside of the local calling area, then you were paying an additional fee per minute for the call. Today, those fees are included as part of your monthly flat rate cell phone bill, but in the late '90s, it was in the range of 10 to 15 cents per minute.

With long-distance rates being what they were, it didn't take long to rack up phone bills of $200 to $250 each month. My first semester on campus, on top of blowing the little money I had moved with, I squandered what remaining financial aid I had left on long-distance phone calls to family and friends.

I'd tell myself that I'd only talk for five or ten minutes so it wouldn't cost that much. But like almost all of my other plans, it was destined to fail from the beginning. Before I knew it, I would talk to someone for a half-hour or more. And usually it was several someones each night.

By the end of my first semester, I was once again broke. I had spent all of the leftover money from my student loans and grants after paying for tuition and books, money that was supposed to be used for things like rent and groceries. To avoid dropping out and going back home, I took a job sacking groceries at a local grocery story for minimum wage. I also applied for another credit card and was approved.

That's right! Even after all of my previous poor credit card behavior, I was able to get approved for another card just a short time later. My credit score must have still been "good enough," right? Wrong! The reality was that my brief credit history showed that while I might have been a risk for an auto or mortgage loan, I was the perfect customer for a credit card company. I had proven that I wasn't bashful about spending and wasn't concerned about paying interest or penalties. Credit card companies knew they could make money off of me and that I'd eventually pay everything back that I borrowed. So just because you may be able to get a credit card after some suspect credit behavior, don't be fooled into thinking that your credit score is "good enough." It probably isn't.

I had also accepted the realization that I was going to have to find a roommate to split living expenses with. I had learned nothing from my struggles prior to moving off to college. Or at least I had not created any positive changes based on what I had learned.

By March of 1999, my second semester, I had moved on from the grocery store after only a few months and was working the front desk at a hotel and making $7.50 per hour, which was far more than I had ever made before. I also had moved into a two-bedroom apartment and found a roommate, a complete stranger, to share it with. As you can imagine, being the introvert I was, this was an extremely awkward and uncomfortable situation for me.

I went to class in the mornings, went home for lunch and some relaxation, and then headed to work at 3:00 pm, getting off at 11:00 pm. By the time I got home, unwound, and fell asleep for class the next morning, there wasn't much studying taking place. My grades were not great, but still good enough to stay in school.

Despite working close to a full-time schedule for the next three years, I continued to take the full amount of financial aid possible even though I had the option to decline some or all of the loans. Because the time to repay the loans seemed far off even though I'd have to begin paying them back and interest would start to accumulate six months after graduating, it felt like free money at the time. I never thought about *not* accepting all of the loans that were offered.

Since I ended up having plenty of money (too much, actually), I came up with another brilliant plan: each semester when my financial aid came in, I could use some of it to by myself a gift. One semester it was an Aiwa stereo system. Another semester, it was a 27" Sony Trinitron television since I had decided my 19" Magnavox needed upgrading and could be moved into my bedroom. There was a trip to Dallas for a weekend to see the Dave Matthews Band followed by the aforementioned tickets and trip to Dallas for the annual Oklahoma–Texas football game a few weeks later.

Now, looking back on what I did, my advice would clearly be to only take the amount of student loans *you absolutely need* to pay for tuition, books, and living expenses. Borrow as little as you possibly have to. Get a part-time or full-time job if your studies will allow so that you can further reduce your need to borrow.

The more loans you take out, the more you have to pay back and the more interest you will end up paying on those loans. Considering that I've been making monthly payments of around $250 per month (including interest) on close to $25,000 in student loan debt for nearly twenty years, I wonder what those items really ended up costing me.

Be careful with financial aid! It's just like with credit cards: be responsible and use it only for what it is intended for. Financial aid is a great tool for those who need it and who would not have access to higher education without it, but don't abuse it like I did.

I now wonder what life would have been like if I had only ended up taking on half the debt that I did. I likely could have paid it off in half the time, saving thousands of dollars, and I would not have been saddled with the monthly payments I still have today.

I highly recommend being as certain as possible that college is what you want to do at the time you commit to taking student loans. Do your best to ensure that you study something that will inspire you and that you will remain passionate about for the long term. Obviously, nobody knows how things will go or how interests might change, but do your best. Don't base your choices on how much money you will make upon graduation. If that is your focus, it increases the likelihood that you will pick a course of study you won't enjoy. Don't worry that you won't be able to afford to pay your student loans back if you don't make a certain amount of money. Once finished with school, you can always apply for an income-driven repayment plan that will make your debt more manageable based on your income.

The point of all this is to avoid the worst-case scenario, one that's even worse how mine turned out: taking out loans for a year or two and then realizing college isn't for you. Then you end up dropping out with thousands of dollars in debt and minimum-wage employment attempting to pay back that debt.

Another bad scenario is realizing two years in that you've chosen the wrong field of study. This happens as we discover new things and learn more about ourselves, but it too is very costly, as you could end up paying back debt for something that never paid you.

Oh, and make sure to pass all of your classes! I failed my economics class during my first semester after moving away from home. It was a three-credit-hour course. With tuition, books, and fees, I would estimate it cost roughly $500 for the class. I earned a D, which is failing, and had to retake the class. Would you like to guess what that cost me in loan interest over these past twenty years? Luckily, student loan interest rates are usually significantly less than other forms of debt, but quickly plugging some numbers into a repayment calculator shows I've paid for that class a couple times over.

Financial aid shenanigans and missteps aside, I managed to finally graduate in December of 2001, four months shy of my twenty-seventh birthday. I was finally a college graduate. Finally ready to make some real money and have everything I had ever dreamed of!

9

An Introduction to Your New Best Friend: Money Management Software

"You must gain control over your money or the lack of it will forever control you."
— **Dave Ramsey**, Radio show host, author, businessman, and creator of Financial Peace University

I spent eight months after graduating looking for a job. I graduated with a Bachelor of Business Administration with a double major in management and management information systems, which is information technology or IT. Graduation was December of 2001, three months after 9/11, one of the worst days in our nation's history. The economy had tanked, people had lost jobs, and the job market was extremely tough, especially for a new college graduate.

I finally landed a job working in data and IT with a salary of $25,000 per year, or roughly $12/hour. Hardly the big payoff I was expecting and hardly a salary that would provide all of the material possessions I thought I was owed.

I spent most of the next five years struggling financially, attempting to achieve big goals with poor planning and execution. I cycled through different roommates so that I could live in a rental house I couldn't afford by myself with few new possessions other than the brand-new 2003 Honda Accord I had bought for myself when my 1983 Accord started to finally give out. It was the second time I had tried to replace my '83 Accord, and neither time could I really afford it. A couple of years earlier, while I was still in college, I was rear-ended at a stop sign. The car was damaged, but repairable for a reasonable price. Instead of doing that, though, I decided to park it and buy something different.

I went to a dealership and purchased a used 1997 Accord that came with a 13% interest rate. Having paid off the credit cards I had maxed out after high school and then having repaired my credit rating due to better credit card behavior in college made that interest rate possible. While I had racked up some new credit card debt with more questionable purchases, I had managed to keep it under control to the point of being able to afford to make payments on time.

About a year later, I put an end to this poorly-thought-out experiment when I sold the '97 Accord because I couldn't afford it and repaired the '83 Accord. I drove it until I got the job after graduation and felt like I was entitled to something new.

The 2003 Accord was the first new car I had ever owned and was my prized possession. I still own it today—it has 260,000 miles on it and is going strong—because of the sentimental value it has for me and because it just makes financial sense. I even replaced the engine with a used one when the original gave out. Spending that $2,700 was better than making monthly payments for a new car! I guess I learned the lesson that it's often better to repair than to replace.

But when repair does not make sense and replacing *is* the best option, consider your options. "Replace" doesn't necessarily have to mean buying brand-new, especially when it comes to a vehicle. In fact, I have only purchased two brand-new vehicles in my life. All of the others were used vehicles and they did the job just as well as brand-new and didn't include the immediate loss of value you experience from driving a new vehicle off the car lot.

You see, as soon as that brand-new vehicle is sold and driven off the lot, it is no longer new—it's used. And people won't pay the same amount for a used car as they will for a new car no matter how little used it is. So who eats that loss? *You.* The original buyer does. Keep that in mind (as well as other costs) when determining between repair, replace with used, or replace with new.

When I first bought the 2003 Accord, between the car payments and my regular living expenses (rent, utilities, groceries, and so forth), I was broke. I was still living paycheck to paycheck with no emergency savings, no retirement savings, and no backup plan if I lost my job.

After a couple of years of work, I decided I was ready to relocate—I wanted to be closer to the people I missed. I decided Tulsa was a good spot. It was only 45 minutes from my parents, an hour and a half from where my brothers lived, and an hour and a half from Norman for when I wanted to go back for a football game. Seemed like a good spot in the middle of everything.

Wanting to give my employer plenty of time to find my

replacement and thinking that I needed *some* time but not too much time to find a job in Tulsa, I gave three months' notice of my last day. I applied for jobs, found an apartment in Tulsa, put down the deposit with the first month's rent, and made all of the necessary moving arrangements.

I never managed to get a job in Tulsa before my scheduled moving day, but that didn't stop me from leaving my job and making the move anyway. I had no job, no savings, a $370-a-month car payment, $350 monthly rent for my new apartment, and $2,000 in credit card debt. How was I supposed to pay for that plus insurance, utilities, gas, groceries, and everything else?

I continued to look for a job in information technology with no luck. A few months passed by, and I finally gave in and took a job with the same hotel chain I had worked for in college. It paid enough to help with gas, groceries, and utilities, but that was about it.

A few months later, I finally landed a job in IT at a car rental company and could now cover all of my expenses. The bad part was that in the eight months it had taken me to find the job, my credit card debt had ballooned from $2,000 to $12,000. I had been paying for almost everything on my credit card: my car payments and insurance, rent, and everything else that the hotel job wasn't covering.

I was now making more money than I ever had and once again set out to eliminate a large credit card debt. I was able to pay $1,000 per month on average and paid off the $12,000 within a year. I was once again free of credit card debt and vowed that it would never happen again.

Three significant things happened toward the end of that five-year stretch that really changed the direction of my life. The first was completing graduate school, where I earned a Master of Business Administration (MBA) degree with a concentration in finance in May of 2007. I had applied a few months after moving to Tulsa, when I couldn't find a job. I had taken on another $20,000 in student loan debt, but my salary after graduating and moving into the finance industry had nearly tripled compared to what I had been making when I finished my undergraduate degree. In addition, studying finance finally taught me what it meant to be financially responsible, both in a business environment and in a personal sense. It was a turning point that I now had to apply to my own life.

Second, I met my new family: my wife and her two sons, who were four and five years old at the time. Our wedding was in August of 2007, three months after I had finished graduate school. If I needed any further incentive to get my act together, this was it. It was one thing to be foolish and irresponsible when it was just me—it was something else to be responsible for the well-being of a family. *My* family.

The weekend of our wedding, I moved from my apartment to the two-bedroom, 1,200-square-foot house she had purchased for herself and the boys a year earlier. (I had actually helped her move into the home, which turned into the beginning of our relationship.) We considered it a starter home, and our main goal was saving for a new home and paying off the $10,000 in credit card debt she brought to the marriage. My wife had very little interest in the details of money management, so she left it to me to figure out. We had big goals, and I had to come up with the supporting smaller goals to get us there: figure out how much to save, how much to pay toward the credit card debt, and where to reduce costs.

Enter the third significant thing. I discovered there were actually money management tools that could help manage personal finances. Software that I could buy and install on our home computer that would allow me to keep track of everything related to personal finance in one place. For someone who was now 32 years old and had struggled with finance for the better part of two decades, it was the most fantastic thing I had ever seen.

I could link our checking account and our credit card accounts together over the Internet and download all of the transactions. I could then create categories of expenses like dining, groceries, gas, different utilities, entertainment, and clothing and then categorize each transaction appropriately to keep track of how much we were spending in each area. As we went along, I added categories for sports, school activities, music lessons, vacations, gifts, health and fitness, grooming (haircuts and pedicures), home improvement, donations, and on and on.

A couple of times a week, I would gather all of our receipts, log into the software, download the transactions, and then go through each receipt categorizing the purchases. Sometimes it was just a one-item purchase and it was straightforward. Other times I might have to divide out the items and sum the amounts and taxes on receipts that contained expenses for multiple categories. It may sound tedious and cumbersome, but it really wasn't. Besides, having access to all of the information that process provided was well worth it!

Speaking of receipts, there is a trend in society now for many retailers to ask if you want a receipt. It seems like when I'm standing in line somewhere and I hear the question asked, about 90% of the time, the customer says no. And every time that happens, I think to myself, *Say yes! Say yes!* Because without that receipt, how are you going to know what you spent your money on? When you download that transaction with five items or more on it, how are you going to know how to categorize those items?

I completely understand reducing paper waste and the desire of companies to reduce costs by reducing the receipts they hand out, but I believe that small piece of paper has great value. I hope *you'll* now see that value, too, if you are one of the many who say "No" to your receipts.

Once all the information was accurately in the software, the magic happened. I could actually run reports and see where all the money was going. How much my wife and I were spending each month on eating out, on entertainment, for clothes, and everything else. We could pull information that was extremely valuable in decision-making. For example, if we wanted to buy a big-ticket item or take a trip, we could examine where we could cut back and by how much so that we could make it happen.

Over time, as the software became more sophisticated, we could also include our retirement and investment accounts as well as debts like our house, automobiles, and student loans. With everything included, the software then calculated a net worth.

To this point, I have left out one key feature of any personal money management software, which is the ability to create a budget. The reason is because this was the last aspect I myself adopted. Even though I was keeping track of all of the expenditures and knew where all of our money was going each month, for several years we didn't take advantage of the budget feature. And, like so many others, we unfortunately missed out on all of its benefits.

We were afraid what we'd find out about ourselves on a

budget, and we didn't want to be restricted in how we spent our money. Other excuses people often use are that they failed with budgeting in the past so they think they'll fail again, they think they don't have enough money for a budget, they think they can keep track of their expenses in their head, or they're just too lazy to do it. There are tons of excuses for why people don't budget, but there is no real reason not to.

A budget is simply a plan for your money based on your income (how much you have coming in) and your expenses (how much you have going out). You decide how your income will be divided up and spent on a monthly basis. A common guideline is what is referred to as the 50-20-30 rule. Fifty percent of your income goes to needs/expenses, 20% goes to savings, and 30% goes to whatever you want. But don't get too caught up in these numbers right now—they're just a starting point and they are different for everyone's unique situation. I'll discuss this in more detail later.

Based on how much you estimate your income to be for the month, you divide it into expense categories based on what you plan to do with it. Some common budget line items for you to consider would be your car payment if you have one, gas for your car, your phone, eating out, and entertainment. If you are already living on your own, you would want to include rent, utilities, and groceries. You probably have other items on your list seeing as everyone's budget is unique.

Decide how much you plan to spend each month in each category. In the event that you have a category or item that isn't paid each month—maybe you are billed every other month, quarterly, or biannually for your auto insurance—then figure out how much you anticipate to be billed for the year and divide it by twelve. For example, if you anticipate the total annual amount due to be $600, then divide it by twelve and budget $50 per month. That way, you will know how much you have to save each month to cover the payment when it is due. If it is a payment that may fluctuate some, you may want to include a little extra each month to cover any potential overages.

As you download transactions and categorize them throughout the month, the software will apply those expenditures to the matching line item in your budget, showing you what you have spent to date and how much you have remaining for the month in each category. But remember, the line items that are *not* paid each month will appear to have an excess amount for the months during which no payment is due. Be careful not to get confused and think that you have extra money available to move to another budget line item!

If you're halfway through the month and you have spent 75% of your entertainment budget, slow down. If you get to the end of the month and have some left, use it to boost your savings. Keep in mind that just because it's available at the end of the month doesn't mean you have to spend it. There's nothing wrong with putting a little extra away for an emergency.

If you go over in a category or two for a month (or even two months), don't stress about it. Sure, the goal is to develop discipline and good habits with your money, but there are other measurements of success or failure than just one month. What are your quarterly budget results? Did you barely overspend two months but then come in way under the third month? If so, you succeeded for the quarter. The same goes for six months and annually.

If you notice a trend where you missed the mark in a category several months in a row and see it beginning to negatively affect your financial well-being, then make an adjustment: bump your budget up a little for that category if you can comfortably reduce spending in another category to balance things out. If you can't find excess funds to cover the increase, then you have no choice but to reduce spending or increase your income to avoid taking on debt.

Despite not creating a budget or taking advantage of that discipline the software could have provided, my wife and I still managed to get enough out of the software to reduce our spending, change our habits (like reducing impulse spending), establish an emergency savings account, and pay down our debt.

Now we use the budgeting feature, too, and what a difference creating and sticking to a budget has made! What was difficult in the beginning—being somewhat restricted and not spending on a whim—is not difficult at all anymore. The pain was short-lived. You know why? Because as afraid as humans are of change, we adapt, and usually very quickly. Don't be afraid! What is initially painful soon becomes comfortable.

You may fear that implementing a budget would be too stressful and hard, but really, it will have the opposite effect. By having a budget, you will reduce your stress immensely by having full control of your financial status, a situation that's made possible by knowing where every penny of your income is going. You will no longer subject yourself to the stress of living paycheck to paycheck or of not having enough for emergencies or unexpected expenses.

I cannot stress enough the value of using a money management tool! It changed everything for me and has probably been the single biggest factor in my financial turnaround. It hasn't made me rich in a financial sense, but it was the start of getting everything that has made me rich in life.

Budgeting is essential to your financial health and can only enhance your ability to make decisions that will improve your financial well-being. But remember, the only way budgeting works at its best and leads to good decision-making is when the data is accurate. That means you have to do your part and put in the effort to make sure that all of your financial data is entered and categorized accurately.

You can do this from a computer or from a smartphone. All of the different providers of these money management tools—and there are many options to choose from—have apps, making it really easy to stay on top of things whether you are at home or on the go. I've found over time that it is easier to download and categorize transactions every couple of days. At times, I have gone as much as two to three weeks between downloads, and waiting that long makes the process seem much more time-consuming and tedious. The easier it feels, the more likely you are to stick to it; the more cumbersome it feels, the more likely you are to put it off or let it go all together. Plus, by downloading your transactions more often, you will always have the most up-to-date and accurate picture of your finances at your fingertips.

Over the years, more and more tools have entered the personal finance management market. After all, it's an issue that impacts all of us and has become a huge problem in our society. There are many suitable options, from the simplest tracking management and budgeting tools to more complex options that offer investing and tax management and online bill payment. Some have a monthly or annual fee and some are free. And there are many places to go online to read reviews about the different options, including the positives and negatives. That way, you can determine which one will be the best fit for your needs and your budget. (Yes, you should consider the cost of budgeting in your budget.)

The software I chose and still use today is a popular one called Quicken. My wife and I have recorded and categorized every single one of our financial transactions since July of 2007. Back then, you could download Quicken onto your computer for a fee and then you could update to a new version a couple of years later for another fee. Today, Quicken is offered online for an annual fee.

A couple of other popular programs include Mint and You Need A Budget (YNAB). Mint offers bill tracking, budget tracking, retirement tracking, and online credit monitoring, all at no cost. YNAB focuses mostly on tracking and budgeting for a monthly fee. YNAB also offers three key rules (which I happen to agree with) to guide you on your journey:

· Rule #1: Give every dollar a job—think, *What should this money do before I am paid again?*

· Rule #2: Embrace your true expenses—think short about today's expenses, but also think long about expenses down the road.

· Rule #3: Roll with the punches—if your budget needs changing, just change it, don't beat yourself up over it.

I am not promoting or recommending any of these options for you. I do not have anything to gain financially from them, and I know nothing of your current financial position to advise you on what is best for you. What I do know from firsthand experience is that regardless of which option you choose, a personal money management tool is critical for your success. Any choice is better than no choice at all!

10

Final Tips

"Fools say that they learn by experience. I prefer to profit by others' experience."

— **Otto von Bismarck**, Responsible for transforming a collection of small German states into the German empire, and Germany's first chancellor

Personal Financial Principles Are the Same No Matter the Income

Whether you make minimum wage for a living or half a million dollars a year, the principles of achieving financial freedom are the same. That's because many of us tend to live paycheck to paycheck and beyond our means regardless of how much money we make.

We try to live a lifestyle above and beyond what the career and life choices we have made will comfortably allow. We sacrifice other important aspects, such as sticking to a budget or saving for emergencies. But no matter what income level your life choices lead you to, do your best to stick to personal financial principles. Stick to that budget no matter how tight it may be! Develop a habit of putting something—anything—into a savings account on a regular basis. Maybe your dream or idea of freedom is to be done with school. Maybe college is not in your plan and you want to go straight into the workforce in the town you've grown up in and get your own place to live. You don't mind that you may make minimum wage or just a little more than that. And let's be clear: every choice is a valid one if it is right for you.

We all make our choices and decide what will make us happy. Every job supports our society in its own way. We need you, no matter what you choose to do for a living. But be willing to accept the lifestyle that goes with the career path you choose.

Don't get caught up in the material things that society says you must have. You don't need a brand-new car—all you need is reliable transportation. That could be buying a used vehicle or taking advantage of public transportation. You could even choose to live close enough to work that you can walk there or ride a bike. You don't need a high-end apartment in a trendy area of town—you need a place that provides safety and security, a place you can call home. You need savings for emergencies.

Someday you may decide you do want to go back to school, whether it's trade school or college. Or maybe you'll decide you want to live in another town, state, or even another country. Goals change, dreams change, and life happens. Be prepared and don't be your own roadblock to fulfilling your dreams.

The same is true if you end up making six figures or more. Imagine that you go to college, work really hard for a few years, impress someone, and earn a great promotion and raise. Or maybe out of high school, you take a sales job and find you are really good at it and end up traveling the country as a sales rep. You get married. You choose to buy a four- or five-bedroom house even though you have no children and it's just the two of you, and your house is in a new neighborhood with a homeowner's association (HOA) and a pool and park exclusively for the residents. You own two brand-new German-engineered automobiles, one for the each of you.

You think you deserve it for all of the hard work you have put in. It's your reward! Plus, your new neighbors own similar types of cars. You've furnished your big, brand-new house with high-end furniture. You have a television in each room of the house even though you never spend time in more than a room or two. You spend Friday and Saturday nights at fancy restaurants with friends. You think you've made it, that you've got it all. But the reality is that you have no savings, you aren't funding your retirement accounts, and you have bills you can't pay until your next check hits your bank account.

You come to realize that you really don't like the career path you have chosen and want something that comes with less stress and less responsibility…but also pays less money. Or you suddenly have a calling in your heart that may result in a reduction in income but can no longer be ignored.

It happens. I know it happens firsthand, and I know others it has happened to as well. The current pastor at the church my family and I attend was an attorney not too long ago. About ten years ago, in his early forties, he decided he could no longer ignore the calling he had to leave the law firm he and his wife shared together and enter the seminary instead. Today he is the lead pastor of his home church, the church he attended prior to his calling and career change.

The point is that no matter the path you choose or the scenario you find yourself in, the rules of having the freedom, flexibility, and quality of life we all desire are the same: don't sacrifice your *quality of life* and everything it entails for your *lifestyle.* Don't handcuff yourself to your current dream, because your dreams will likely change throughout your life.

Make Experiences and Not Possessions Your Goals

It is better to spend your money on experiences as opposed to possessions. I had never thought of this until I read about it. It made perfect sense. I began to think about all of the experiences I remembered most from my childhood and the fantastic things I have been lucky enough to experience so far as an adult.

I then began to think about the possessions I had as a child and the ones I acquired as an adult. They couldn't begin to compare with the joy and fond memories that each experience had brought me. The experiences are memories I'll have for the rest of my life! The possessions hardly inspired any emotion at all.

Think about it for just a moment. What are the things you remember most from your childhood? Is it the toys or the clothes or any other possessions you had or still have? Or is it the birthday parties, the vacations, the trips to the park or swimming pool, going to see a movie, etc.?

The fun things we experience as children vary for all of us based on what our parents had the ability to provide, but I'm willing to bet that big or small, you have experiences that bring happiness and warmth every time you think back to them. And I'll bet you cannot say the same for many particular possessions. I know I can't.

Thinking back to my childhood, I can remember very few

possessions I had and even fewer that really mattered or meant anything to me. But what I do remember fondly are the sports I played, the trips to Kansas City to see the Royals play, summers going to our city swimming pool as many times a day as I wanted to because we had seasonal passes, and vacations.

One of my greatest memories from my childhood was when one of my earliest baseball teams won the city championship. We played 16 games that season and finished with a record of 14-1-1, with the tie being a result of weather. I believe I was seven or eight years old at the time. The coaches (one of them being my dad) gave the team a choice: we could each have a trophy to celebrate the championship or we as a team could go to Kansas City to attend a Royals game.

Thankfully, the team chose the baseball game. I still remember it today, nearly forty years later. Driving four hours to the stadium in a van with my teammates on a Saturday morning, sitting in the stands on a hot summer day looking down at the green artificial turf, watching my baseball hero George Brett play against the Baltimore Orioles *in person* for the first time, and then driving home that night.

As for the trophy that never was, I don't miss it at all. In fact, I was fortunate enough to play for another city championship team a few years later, and I do still have a trophy for that. I recently got it out of a box in my attic where it had been packed away more than twenty years ago. I have obviously still valued it enough to keep it all of these years, but no doubt I would have traded it for another trip to see a professional baseball game with my teammates.

I'm trying to pass this mindset on to my children. My seven-year-old son recently had a birthday. He invited a few friends over and we took them and our family to a minor league baseball game. The kids had all the typical food and played at the splash pad and park in the outfield seating. My son even got one of the few balls that are tossed out to the fans between innings. He and everyone else had a great time.

A few days later, he remarked that he hadn't gotten many toys for his birthday, which was true. We spent what was in our budget for his birthday on the baseball game. I am confident that in time the thought of the toys he missed out on will fade, but the memories of his birthday spent at the baseball game will remain.

I am fairly certain that when I look back thirty years from now, what will spark the warmth of fond memories will not be the type of cars I drove or how big the TVs in the house were. The spark will come from experiences like the week we spent in Ireland a few years ago, like when we took the kids to Washington, D.C. and Yellowstone National Park and Royals games.

So this should be your focus now: spend less on possessions and instead use your financial resources to create experiences that will last a lifetime. The memories of the possessions won't stand the test of time, but the memories of your experiences most certainly will.

Be Prepared When Opportunity Knocks

Have you ever been invited to do something you really wanted to do but you had to say no because you had just spent your money on something else? Or maybe someone was looking to get rid of something and offered it to you for a great deal, but you didn't have the money at the time? If it hasn't happened yet, it likely will at some point. It's not a good feeling. While the thought of things missed out on early in life may sting for a short time, it's nothing compared to the disappointment of the more significant missed opportunities you may experience in the future if you aren't prepared with a solid financial plan no matter your income.

For many of us, there is a chance that at some moment in the future, opportunity will knock. A friend, a family member, somebody, anybody will pop up out of the blue with an opportunity for you. But it's only there for the taking *if* you are prepared, *if* you have the necessary resources to take advantage of it.

For example, an old friend you haven't spoken to in years calls you up and says he has a great job opportunity for you…but it will require you to relocate with no financial assistance to help you make the move. Unfortunately, you have failed to save any of your earnings, instead squandering it all on material possessions.

Or the economy goes into a tailspin and the stock market crashes as it did during the great recession of 2008. At that time, I had just started working at Dollar Thrifty Automotive Group, a car rental company that owned the Dollar and Thrifty brands. I was hired as a contractor, meaning I had no benefits and was paid hourly. As the economy continued to worsen in the two months after I was hired and layoffs were announced, I was sure I would be gone. But as it turned out, because I was a contractor, I was cheaper to keep around than someone with benefits like medical insurance and a matching 401k, so I survived the cuts.

The company's stock price had tanked and was trading at less than $1 per share. It was the perfect time to buy. As the saying goes, "Buy low and sell high," and things were about as low as they could get. Of course, there was risk. I could still lose my job, my wife could lose her job, we could *both* end up unemployed. And if you lost your job at that time, forget about finding another one for a while.

While there was greater risk at that time, there is risk in any investment, whether it be investing in the stock market, stepping out to start your own business, pursuing a real estate opportunity, or taking up a friend's invitation to go into business together. As they say, "No risk, no reward."

But there was one big problem preventing me from taking advantage of such an opportunity: my wife and I were not financially prepared to do so. While we were making more money than we ever had, we were also spending more on material possessions and did not have anything saved that we could invest.

As it turned out, the company survived, the economy recovered (as is always the case), and neither my wife nor I ever lost our jobs. Nearly four years later, in August of 2012 and while I was still with the company, Hertz, a rival car rental company and the biggest in the industry, agreed to buy Dollar Thrifty for $2.3 billion, or about $87.50 per share.

Imagine the what-ifs. What if we had been prepared to take advantage of the opportunity? What if we could have purchased five thousand shares at $1 each? What if we could have sold those shares for $87.50 each and made a profit of more than $430,000?

I get that is a lot of ifs. There's always the chance we would have sold much earlier, when maybe the stock had only increased to $10 or $20 per share. Maybe we wouldn't have netted the life-changing profit mentioned above, but still, a nice profit could have been had nonetheless.

My point is, always be prepared for opportunity. And the

only way to do that is by managing your finances wisely, not overextending yourself on things you don't need, and saving for when that opportunity that's too good to pass up finally knocks. Because it most definitely will.

Always Be Prepared! Don't Get Caught Off Guard By the "Unexpected"

"Always be prepared!" You've probably heard that many times. Remember your new best friend the money management software? One of the best things about using a money management tool is how it can prepare you for the unexpected. It won't completely eliminate unpredictability when it comes to your finances, but it will most definitely reduce the chances of you getting caught with your guard down.

Since I began tracking all of our expenses in 2007, I have been able to identify trends in spending, even unexpected costs such as medical expenses and home and auto maintenance costs. This has helped us stay more prepared than we would have been otherwise. But I didn't always take advantage of the data I had at my fingertips. Even though I spent a lot of time downloading and categorizing transactions, I didn't always use the information to create and stick to a budget.

It was just before Christmas a few years ago when I realized what I had been missing out on. Early that December, my wife unexpectedly needed some dental work that ended up costing us $518. For many people, with the added pressure of the holiday season, the timing would have been horrible.

Out of curiosity, to see if there was any way we could have possibly planned for such an expense, I decided to open our tracking software and run a report of our annual out-of-pocket dental and medical costs for each year since I had begun categorizing all of our expenses. What I found was truly amazing to me: over the previous nine years, we had averaged annual out-of-pocket expenses of $2,968.37 for dental and medical. The dental payment we had just made pushed our total to $3,129.11 for that year, making a difference of only $160.74.

It was an unexpected expense that we could have been better prepared to absorb. While there is no way to predict if or when a dental or medical need may arise or how small or big of an expense it may be, the fact is, if we had used the data that was available to us, we easily could have created a budget for the category that would have allowed us to be better prepared.

All I had to do at the beginning of the year was divide the $2,968.37 by 12 months to create an average monthly budget of $247.36 for the category. Then when December rolled around, I could have updated that month's budget for the remaining amount that had not been spent. In this example, that would have been $357.26. It wouldn't have allowed us to fully plan for an expense of $518, but nothing is 100%. At the very least, it would have allowed us to be more prepared than we were and not have to dip into our emergency fund quite as much. See how simple that is?

One of the things I think we all dread the most is taking our vehicle in for some routine maintenance like an oil change and a tire rotation and being told we need new tires or something else. This happened to us one morning when I took our car in for an oil change before we were scheduled to take a trip. I was prepared for a $35 oil change and a free tire rotation. Instead, I was told that our current set of 80,000-mile tires had 90,000 miles on them and needed to be replaced. After realizing I had no choice due to safety reasons and after the feeling of surprise had worn off, I agreed. On my way home, I called my wife and told her that the $35 oil change had turned into an oil change, a new set of tires, and an alignment at a cost of $1,022.

I soon realized that just as was the case with the dental expense, the information I would have needed to plan for this expense was right in front of me. When making our budget for the year, all I had to do was look back and find the last time we had bought tires for that vehicle. Combining that information with the fact that I knew we had put about 30,000 miles per year on our car, I could have easily figured out that new tires would be needed sometime during the current year. It was all right there, right in front of me! We could have been better prepared for that expense.

Whether we realize it or not, we spend a large amount of time and resources attempting to reduce risk in our lives. We buy medical, dental, auto, homeowner's, renter's, and life insurance. We use alarm clocks because we don't want to risk being late. But for some reason, most of us fail to take the simple steps that lead to reducing the risk of getting hit with a large, unexpected financial expense.

Don't be one of the 40% of Americans who would have difficulty covering a $400 surprise bill! Just consult your friend the money management software—it has all the answers. And then enjoy the stress release of being prepared.

Live Your Best Life Now While Preparing for the Future

We all know the person who lives in the moment, flying by the seat of their pants. They give no regard to tomorrow, next week, next month, next year, or any time in the future. Their only goal is to live life to the fullest, doing anything and everything they want in the moment. They have no plans or intentions of saving anything—they'll worry about their future when it's suddenly their present.

We also know the person who is a real penny-pincher and saves everything for that time in the future when they no longer have to work and can enjoy the fruits of their labor. They'll do everything they've ever dreamed of then, when they're free from any other responsibilities. They assume that they will still be able to physically do the things they want and that the important people in their life will still be there able to enjoy those times with them.

I believe we should seek a middle ground between those two scenarios. Our focus should be on living the best possible life we can *now* while at the same time we're preparing and planning for the future when we no longer want to earn an income. And despite what many personal financial gurus preach, spending now and saving for the future are not independent of each other. They can actually be done at the same time. It's a balancing act that can be easily accomplished.

Why is this middle ground the best spot? Because it's the place where we can live a great and satisfying life in our youth and maintain that same lifestyle or even improve upon it as we age. Nobody wants to end up where they can no longer earn enough to support the lifestyle to which they have become accustomed. No one wants to no longer be able to afford their home and have to downgrade to something less. No one wants to no longer be able to afford to travel the way they were accustomed to traveling or not be able to see their friends and family as often as they once did. But that's where some people wind up—they can no longer afford entertainment or hobbies, and they may not be able to cross off bucket list items they had been putting off for that future date.

Of course, at some point, we may decide that we no longer want those things. We may get tired of taking care of a yard or no longer need as much space as we once did, but let that be a choice and not something that is dictated to you. Don't let that happen because you were so focused on the here and now.

Take advantage of your youth! With careful planning and responsible financial management as your guide, do the things you want to do. Occasionally reward yourself for successfully staying within your budget—that will remind you that the sacrifices you have made are worth it. Occasional (and reasonable) rewards will provide the positive reinforcement to stay the course.

If you desire and are responsibly able to, travel the world, go out with friends, and enjoy life. But don't sacrifice your future by neglecting to save and plan for it. Find that middle ground where you can live a satisfying life today while at the same time you prepare to transition into different stages when you no longer want to work.

Don't Go It Alone

If there is a single thing you take away from this book, let it be this: don't try to do this all on your own. If I'm really being honest with myself and pinning my struggles on the single biggest mistake I made, that mistake would be that I didn't ask for help. Looking back, that was partially because I didn't want anyone else to know what I was doing, but I also thought that the only thing I needed was me. I thought I was smart enough to figure things out by myself.

As kids, we don't yet know about or have a full understanding of the skills and tools we need to successfully transition to adulthood. We may think we know, but we truly don't. And when experienced people offer us advice, we tend to ignore it or not take it seriously. It's a natural process and why so many of us end up learning the hard way. And while it may be natural, it's still a choice we make, and it's still one of our single biggest mistakes.

While some of us truly have no one qualified to really help us, most of us choose that path of independence and go it alone. Some of us don't trust the people around us. Some of us are just stubborn. And some of us think we're smart enough to figure things out on our own. This way of thinking is a recipe for disaster, one that will lead to difficult times ahead.

I hope you have the opportunity to take a financial literacy course in school. It is the single most important class you could ever take! Forget math, science, or anything else—financial literacy is the one. In several states (including Oklahoma, where I live), passing a financial literacy class is now required to complete high school graduation. If you are one of the lucky ones in a state where this is the case, embrace it! Grab on to it, take everything from it you possibly can, and apply it to your life *immediately*. If it is not currently available to you, I hope it will be in the very near future.

If you are not getting this class at school, go out and find it. Educate yourself using the tons of resources on the Internet. All you have to do is Google any personal finance topic, and you will find everything you need to get informed. There are government resources like MyMoney.gov that provide valuable information and links to other resources.

Reach out to someone close to you whom you believe has exhibited sound money management in their own life. You will have to ask them questions; basically, you'll need to interview them, since there is no way to tell who's good with money by just looking at what a person has. Some questions might be: Do they have a budget they stick to? Do they use a money management tool? How do they decide when it's a good idea to buy something they want, and how would they would pay for an emergency today? If someone really practices sound financial principles like what we've discussed and wants to help others do the same, they should have no problem answering questions like these.

Once you've created an account with an online money management tool, ask that same person for guidance if you are unsure about the next steps you should take. Ask them to help you open up a retirement savings account. Find someone you feel comfortable bouncing purchasing decisions off of. **I can't stress how important it is to get off on the right foot and establish good habits from the beginning.**

You have no excuse! Great information is easier to find now than ever before, and there are more helpful resources available than ever before. All you have to do is make the choice to take advantage of those resources! I promise, you'll thank yourself later.

Implement the 50-20-30 ~~Rule~~ Guideline (or some variation) and Take Advantage of Automation

Do whatever it takes to safeguard yourself from yourself. Often times, even though we may know what is best for ourselves at a young age and what we need to do to stay the course, we still lack the discipline to do that or we find a way to create chaos and make things more difficult than they need to be. This is especially true when it comes to managing money.

There are two things you can do to help ensure that you stay the course with your money. Implement the 50-20-

30 guideline—or some variation that makes sense for your financial situation—and take advantage of the automation that our financial institutions now make available to us.

As I mentioned earlier when we were discussing budgeting, the 50-20-30 guideline is a common starting point for dividing up your money and ensuring that it gets where it needs to go. That's where 50% of your monthly income goes toward needs or expenses, 20% goes into savings for things like emergencies, and the last 30% goes to whatever you want to spend it on.

For some, though, allocating 50% to expenses may not be enough. Maybe you've just graduated from high school or college and have entered the work force and are earning an entry-level salary. You might not be making enough for 50% of your income to allow you to live in a safe place with reliable transportation *and* still have enough to cover all of your other expenses. Or maybe your job does not offer assistance with medical insurance and you have to cover the entire expense yourself. In this case, you may need to modify the formula to 60-20-20, or 70-15-15, or even 80-10-10.

For others, 20% to savings may not be enough. With more and more people choosing to freelance for the freedom and flexibility it provides or because they can't find suitable employment, they may need to save more for times when work slows down or dries up all together. Freelancers do not receive benefits such as unemployment assistance when they lose a job. For these reasons, your formula may be adjusted to 50-30-20 or 50-40-10.

Whatever the modification may be, always practice the habit of putting something consistent into savings no matter how small it may be. As your career progresses or new opportunities for increased income arise, you can adjust the formula, with

50-20-30 being your eventual target. But remember, these numbers are never set in stone and can be changed at any time based on your income and goals.

To set this up so that it works automatically for you, open a checking account that your paycheck or income will be directly deposited into. Most banks will allow you to customize or personalize your accounts, so name this account "income." Then open two additional checking accounts called "expenses" and "spending" (or whatever you want to call them). Last, open a savings account called—you guessed it—"savings."

Most of the large financial institutions like Chase, Bank of America, Citibank, etc. have no limit on the number of accounts you can open. Many banks also offer accounts with no fees attached and no minimum balance requirements. If there are fees, most institutions offer fee waivers that are not too difficult to qualify for. You'll just have to do some minor research to find a bank that's the best fit for you.

Every time money is deposited into your income account, transfer the funds to your other three accounts in the correct percentages. Remember: 50% to expenses, 20% to savings, and 30% to spending. From the expenses account, you can set up autopay transactions for your car payment if you have one, your car insurance payment, your phone payment, and anything else you are required to pay for regularly. That's it. Your expenses account is hands-off. Same goes for your savings account: it is hands-off until there is an emergency or you need to pay for whatever you have been saving it for.

The only account you will need a debit card for is your spending account. That is the only account you will actually touch on a regular basis and initiate transactions from after your auto payments are set up for your expense account. If you totally deplete your spending account, there is no more spending until your next deposit has come in. That is, unless you have a credit card, and we have already discussed the risks associated with that.

You may find that you actually need more than 50% to go to your expense account. There are a couple of reasons for this. The first, that 50% might not be enough to cover all of your expenses for the month. If that is the case, increase your expense percentage and decrease your spending percentage. Savings should always stay the same (or better yet, increase). It should never decrease.

The second reason is that your income might fluctuate from month to month. That would likely occur because you are an hourly employee and the number of hours you work fluctuates. Some weeks you may work less than full-time; other weeks you may work overtime. If this is the case, you would want to bump up the percentage that goes into your expense account to maybe 55 or 60%. This way, you will create a cushion so that your expenses will always be covered even in the months where you don't work as much. And where will that increase to your expense account come from? Right—from your spending account. I can't say this enough: never adjust your savings downward!

This system makes sure that you take care of your expenses and savings first and reduces the need for you to touch your money. When all of your money goes into one account and everything is spent from it, what most likely happens is we pay for our expenses and then spend the rest on ourselves. It ends up as 50-50 without the savings. But if you use the 50-20-30 guideline, you are ensuring that you actually have a savings account and are funding it first.

Don't Put Off Planning for Retirement

Up to this point, I've only mentioned retirement in passing. I realize it doesn't seem important now and is a lifetime away for you, but it really is something you should be preparing for in a financial sense today or in the very near future, so stick with me here.

According to the Nationwide Retirement Institute (NRI), the average American does not begin saving for retirement until the age of thirty-one. In my case, it was even later. Imagine what a difference thirteen years or more (assuming you start at age eighteen or earlier) would make! There is no reason why every teen or young adult can't be extremely financially comfortable in retirement if they start investing in a retirement account today.

Don't believe me? Check out these numbers from NRI that show the difference between starting your retirement investing at age twenty-three and at age thirty-one. Someone who begins investing $50 every pay period at age twenty-three ends up with $217,150 at age sixty-five, or retirement age. That's compared to $128,578 for someone that starts investing the same amount at age thirty-one (assuming a 6% rate of return).

For a $100 investment per pay period, the amounts jump to $434,299 for someone starting at twenty-three compared to $257,156 for someone starting at age thirty-one (assuming the same 6% rate of return). Whether you are investing $50 per pay period or $100, according to the data, your retirement account will be much greater if you begin investing sooner rather than later.

Now consider a couple other things. What if you start at age eighteen? Or even earlier? Yes, a minor can begin putting money into a retirement account with the help of a parent or other adult. Ask somebody to help you. And what if you increase the amount of money you put into your account as your career progresses and your income increases? Maybe you go from putting in $100 per pay period to $200 to $500. Getting the idea?

And how does it end up being worth so much more than what you put into it? When you open a retirement account, the money you contribute to it is used to buy investments of your choosing, such as stocks and mutual funds. Over time, those investments increase in value (as well as the other investments you purchase) as you continue to make deposits into the account. (Those are called "contributions.") In addition to the gains your investments make, your investment(s) may also earn dividends or interest. Those earnings are then reinvested and used to buy additional securities, resulting in even more earnings. That process is referred to as "compounding."

The more deposits or contributions you make to your account, the more you stand to gain. As long as you remain responsible as you earn more money, you will be able to invest more into retirement. So like I said, there is no reason why you can't be extremely comfortable in retirement from a financial sense.

If you are eighteen or older and are ready to start a retirement account, simply go online and choose an investment company. There are many to choose from, and you can research reviews of the services, fees, and types of investments they offer before making your selection. Once you've decided which company to go with, complete the forms to open either a traditional or a Roth IRA.

Both of these IRAs offer great retirement savings options, but they do have differences regarding the tax impacts. For young adults (most of whom are usually in a lower tax bracket), the advantage of the tax deductions offered for traditional IRA contributions are not that significant. For that reason, the Roth IRA usually makes more sense. With the Roth IRA, you can withdraw contributions any time without penalty, you can withdraw earnings up to $10,000 without penalty after five years for a first-time home purchase or to pay for college, and withdrawals made during retirement are tax-free. This last part is significant given that you will likely be in a higher tax bracket at the time of retirement than you were in your early earning years. Whichever you choose, make sure you understand the differences before investing so that you choose the one that is right for you.

Then it's just a matter of making your investment choices and making your contributions, which you can set up automatically by selecting the account to draw them from, the date, and how often. Then you just forget about it. It really is that simple.

11

The End Game: Where It All Leads

"The goal isn't more money. The goal is living life on your terms."
 –**Chris Brogan**, author, journalist, marketing consultant, and speaker about social media marketing

At this point, you might be asking yourself, "What's the end game? Where is this all going to lead?" The way I see it, you have a couple of options: you can ignore everything I've discussed, take your chances, and hope you right the ship someday (who knows how far down the road), or you can take advice from me and those around you to get on the right track *now* and open up your world to it becoming whatever you want it to be.

There's no getting around it: responsible financial management is the *only* way to unlock the door to financial freedom and everything that comes with it. You don't have to be one of the millions living paycheck to paycheck or trapped in a job you can't stand in order to maintain a certain lifestyle you've envisioned for yourself. All you have to do is make sound financial choices. And those choices will give you the ability to make decisions regarding any aspect of your life without stress or worry.

During the time I spent at home searching for the right job, my wife was offered a new job, but not just *any* job. It was something she had been working toward for years; it really was a dream job. She would be leading her own nonprofit organization, which would require more commitment than anything she had done before.

In the past, my jobs had always paid quite a bit more than hers had, while her jobs had always offered her greater flexibility than mine offered me. Based on this, any required time away from work for family reasons always fell on her. She could work from home when something with the kids required it, do all of the doctor appointments with the kids, leave the office if someone had to be picked up early from school, etc. But with her new opportunity, much of that flexibility would be lost.

As I continued my job search, I began to examine my situation and my feelings about the direction of my career. I realized that doing a job for someone else from home wasn't the solution—I would still be miserable. Whether or not it was really the case, it felt like it was now or never to get out of corporate America.

I opened up our money management software and began to thoroughly review our finances. I found that if we were willing to make a better effort to stick to our budget, we had plenty of opportunities to reduce our spending to the point that I would be able to give up having a job and could instead be a stay-at-home dad so that my wife could take her dream job.

While we could reduce some of our spending categories

significantly or altogether, there were of course things that would likely never go away, like utilities, food, gas, kid's activities, medical bills, insurance, pet bills, etc. But even some of those expenses could be reduced. Our three automobiles were paid for, we had no credit card debt, and we had recently paid off my wife's student loans. Only our mortgage payment and my student loans still remained. As our family's primary money manager, I had come a long way in the past ten years. I had finally become financially responsible! We were in a position that allowed me to walk away from a $75,000 annual income with no need to replace it. And if you're thinking that my wife's new job was making up for that, it wasn't. As far as salary went, it was a lateral move.

Remember back at the beginning of the book when I mentioned two goals I had as a kid? The first was college and the second was to someday run my own business. Well, this was it. Only over time—as I began to learn and understand what I really wanted from life—did the goal of running my own business broaden to doing my own thing, meaning working for myself in some capacity but not necessarily in a business sense.

When I say "working for myself," I don't mean a job where I'm required to do something for someone else with certain stipulations stating what I will deliver and what I will get paid (a contractor, so to speak). I mean doing something meaningful to me that really isn't a job at all, because it's on my terms and something I love doing.

I did some soul-searching, trying to discover what I was good at, what value I had to offer people, and what I would really enjoy doing. Ironically, I realized what I was good at doing and what I wanted to do was help people struggling with their personal finances. As it turns out, I had become pretty good at this finance thing—I had a financial education and work experience, and considering everything I had put myself through, it was a very personal subject to me.

So I started offering financial coaching services to help people right their own ship and improve their quality of life through better personal money management. In addition, I now share my lessons learned by voluntarily speaking to high school students about my own missteps and lessons learned. I also share those hard-won insights through writing. At this stage, whether I make any money from doing this is irrelevant. It's not a job; it's my work.

Again, what's the point of all of this? The point is a simple yet elusive one for most of us: if we can learn good spending habits and follow a few simple concepts of personal money management (follow a budget, create an emergency fund and savings, limit credit card use, and invest in a retirement account), we can live the quality of life we deserve.

I'm now forty-four years old and have come a long way from where I started.

What do you want for yourself? Maybe you want to retire in your thirties or forties to spend more time with your family, travel the world, give back by volunteering, or doing any number of things. There's no rule that says you have to work until the current retirement age of sixty-six or sixty-seven.

Many people will tell you that making mistakes, learning on your own the hard way, and overcoming obstacles through lessons learned is what life is all about. They'll say it means more when you figure things out yourself; they'll say that way, you'll have an appreciation you otherwise wouldn't. Yes, I'm a perfect example of that. But it doesn't have to be that way.

I am lucky. I was raised in a way and experienced things in

my early life that allowed me to develop the perseverance to struggle through and come out the other side the better for it. But at what cost?

How much money did I leave on the table by going to college late and not graduating until I was almost twenty-seven? I would guess somewhere between $100,000 and $200,000. What might my retirement account look like today had I started when I was eighteen as opposed to much later? And what about the stress and worry my financial irresponsibility created? You don't have to do what I did or what millions of others are doing. You don't have to struggle financially and do everything the hard way. You can choose right now to learn from my mistakes and take the easier path.

So what's stopping you? What's holding you back? If you know you need to make changes, if you know you need to turn bad habits into good ones or set up new processes for managing your money better, then get started. Don't let another day go by without making even the slightest progress toward your new financial future. If you're just starting out on your financial journey, then be sure to set out on the right path from the very beginning by refusing to let bad habits take hold and prevent you from reaching your goals.

Lastly, no matter where you are at, don't ever forget that it is never too late to right the ship! You *can* overcome your mistakes, improve your quality of life, and financially free yourself.

Acknowledgements

When I first left behind my career and set out to redefine what I wanted my life's work to look like going forward, I never imagined it would lead me to writing a book. And without the freedom, flexibility, and time I needed to find my way, I never would have ultimately ended up with the idea to do so. For that, I have to first and foremost thank my wife Chris. I am so grateful to have someone who has always believed in me and whose trust and faith in me has never wavered! I can't tell you how great it is to have a partner who values your happiness as much as (or even more) than you do.

Thanks so much to my children for being as understanding as they could at their age when daddy was choosing to spend so much time in the office in front of his computer instead of spending time with them. I promise to make it up to you.

Thank you to my mom and dad for instilling in me the values of perseverance and resilience to face adversity and challenge head-on and never give up.

I learned very early on that there was no way that I could possibly complete this project by myself. The team of professionals who helped me get it done were invaluable. Thanks to my editors, Beth Dorward and Lisa Howard, for their effort and guidance in helping me get my message out. I couldn't have found any better. Thank you to Laura Duffy for her creativity and skills in creating the cover design for this book.

And finally, a great big thanks to my friends and family: Tom Blubaugh, Holly Cinocca, Zach Mendez, and my wife Chris, who trudged through the early drafts, providing honest feedback and positive support that kept me going.

About the Author

Brian Siemens is a financial ~~coach~~ *educator* and public speaker. Brian lives outside of Tulsa with his wife, three children, two foster children, three dogs, and two cats. Brian also has two adult stepsons.

Prior to becoming a writer, Brian worked in information technology and finance for several Fortune 1000 companies. But without a doubt, his favorite "job" has been being a stay-at-home dad as well as a writer and speaker to high school students about personal finance.

Brian attended the University of Oklahoma (Go Sooners!) and received a Bachelor of Business Administration, majoring in management and management information systems. After working for a few years, he went back to school at Oral Roberts University and earned a Master of Business Administration with a finance concentration.

In his free time, Brian enjoys exercising, reading, traveling, and spending time with his kids, whether it's jumping on the trampoline, swimming, shooting hoops, having family game night, or watching them play sports.

You can connect with me on:
- https://www.briansiemens.com
- https://twitter.com/brian_siemens

www.ingramcontent.com/pod-product-compliance
Lightning Source LLC
Chambersburg PA
CBHW071902070526
44583CB00016B/1812